MINDFUL QUARTERBACKING

A Playbook for the Quarterback's Mind

Marcus A. Mayo

ISBN: 978-1-60679-375-6
Library of Congress Control Number: 2016961912
Book layout: Cheery Sugabo
Cover design: Cheery Sugabo
Front cover photo: Gary Marshall/Blackfoot Media Group

Coaches Choice
P.O. Box 1828
Monterey, CA 93942
www.coacheschoice.com

Dedication

Dedicated to:

The Quarterback Position

and

The Game of Football

To My Family

To my entire family tree, and all who have passed away, I love and appreciate each and every single one of you. To those who are living and all future members long after I am gone, I love and appreciate each and every single one of you also. Always follow your heart, treat people the right way, show compassion, be forgiving, strive to find good in others even when it's hard, provide second chances, keep your word, don't judge or assume, live with passion, have fun, laugh, have an imagination, dream big, be creative, be humble, never choose money over happiness, stay kind to those who mistreat you and try to stop you, choose love over hate, ignore the naysayers, remain a fierce competitor, embrace the challenges life presents, embrace what is unfair, fight against the odds with tremendous will power and focus, smile, live in the present moment, always be yourself, and always find a way to triumph. It's what we do!

Prayer. Patience. Perseverance. Progress.

Acknowledgments

Thank you to my entire family who has been by my side through all the ups and downs of this profession. I love you all.

Thank you to all of the coaches I know who have always genuinely had my best interest at heart, have treated me fairly and justly, have helped me grow as a coach, and have wanted me to succeed. You know who you are. Thank you to all of the players I have coached; you are the reason I love my job. Thank you to all of the coaches who have written books and shared their work; it is because of you that people like me can start from scratch and make a career in coaching. I hope this book can help you like your work has helped me.

Special thanks to the following people:

Chris Beatty
Fenton Cheeks
Brian Backus
Adam Stull
Bill Mountjoy
Troy Taylor
Jarod Dodson
Heron O'Neal
Ronnie Brown
Billy Cook
Franklin Craig
Dave Reeves
Justin Bernhardt
Jimmy Beal
Mark Newton
Gary Riekes
Dane Oliver
Pete Joseph
Craig Mettler
Jordan Graham
Adam Scolatti
Dr. Charles Palmer
Mike Van Diest
Jim Hogan
Nick Howlett
Joe Dunning
Mason Siddick
Tyler Emmert
Alex Kastens
Will Cherry
Ethan Vaughn
Ashley Meyers
Sean Doherty
Kristina Kmetekova
Ali Graves
Darrel Williams
Ahmad Mubarak
Jane McNeill
Kat Lee Reyes
Frank Rock
Shawn Claybon
Daniel Garcia
Becky Hawkins
Amara Diakite
Francis Seilenga
Diana Barrera
Keyanna Crawford
Kevin Brown
Derek Gabriel
John Gonzalez
Tracy Graham
Greg Graham
Sara Campbell
Patrick O'Connor
Dr. Jon Kabat-Zinn
Helen Russette
Devon Marcille
Dr. Brad Clough
Bernie Gantert
Melanie Hoell
Jana King
Dr. Paul Dietrich
Mouse Davis
June Jones
Jeff Reinebold
Dan Morrison
J. David Miller
Carlos Barocio-Leon
Dr. Michael Gervais
Christina Costelo
Dr. Shauna Shapiro
Salvatore Ferrera
Mélodie Teruel-Vaissière
Diane Mutschall
Dr. Nathaniel Levtow
Jeuletta Taylor
Daisy Valencia
Mike Bowler Jr.
Stefan Doss
Rigoberto Lopez
Joseph Gray
Ryun Nadeau
Bobby Winston III
Ray Perkins
Kristy Kees
Jeremy Warren
John Mangrum
Melli O'Brien

In Memory of Coach Fenton Cheeks

"A boy comes to me with a spark of interest,
I feed the spark, and it becomes a flame.
I feed the flame, and it becomes a fire.
I feed the fire, and it becomes a roaring blaze."

–Cus D'Amato

Thank you, Coach.
You are truly missed.

Contents

Introduction

Welcome to Mindful Quarterbacking

"The practice of applying Mindfulness to the art of Quarterbacking to assist in obtaining and maintaining optimal performance."

—Mindful Quarterbacking

Mindful Quarterbacking (M-QB) is about creating a Quarterback lifestyle that will allow Quarterbacks to be in the present moment at all times, while competing on the football field and while away from the football field.

Many programs have systems in place that tell him what the defense is, what drops to take, the reads, where to go with the ball, how to throw the ball, and so forth. Although those things are helpful to the art of Quarterbacking, the most important element to playing the toughest position in sports goes beyond schematics and is often overlooked.

Mindful Quarterbacking will help train Quarterbacks to be in the present moment at all times, which will allow them to be coached by their coaches at an optimal level and in turn take their performance to an optimal level.

Mindful Quarterbacking will help Quarterbacks to identify and be themselves (authentic self) and how to effectively handle everyday distractions at any given time. Mindful Quarterbacking will help by enhancing a Quarterback's positive state of mind and give him the confidence that he can handle all distractions and obstacles that come his way in a positive and productive manner.

- How can he handle the negative self-talk that enters his mind at any given moment?
- How can he focus purely on the task at hand without letting the past or future to enter his thoughts; not just on the field, but also away from the field? For example: academics, life at home and life with peers.
- How can he handle situations where the offensive scheme is just not clicking?
- How can he handle a hostile environment?
- How can he handle critical game situations?
- How can he better handle getting hit, sacked, and knocked down play after play after play?
- How can he better handle playing in unwelcoming weather conditions?
- How can he improve his leadership?

- How can he better handle criticism?
- How can he better handle setbacks?

Those examples are just a few of the many questions and circumstances for which this playbook has the answers.

Mindful Quarterbacking will cover many different topics. With practice, a Mindful Quarterback may experience what many describe as a state of flow or being in the zone, but that is not something that can be forced—just experienced and experienced with continuous practice. The main objective is to make being fully present a part of every snap and everyday living, which will enhance the Quarterback's chances of success in every area of life off and on the field.

It's important to remember that Mindful Quarterbacking is a practice that provides Quarterbacks a lifestyle and will assist in maximizing the art of Quarterbacking. The more a Quarterback practices, the better the results will be. This playbook can always be of assistance as long as you want it to be.

"It's all about the now."

—Marcus Mayo

The Quarterback Position

The first thing you may have noticed in this book is that each time you see the word "Quarterback," it is capitalized, as it should be, given that it is the most important job in sports. Football is a team game, and it is the greatest team game in the history of sports. However, a team's success is obtained by every individual on the field doing their individual job. The Quarterback position is the most demanding and challenging position in the history of sports. No position in the history of sports requires a player to command the number of people they command, process as much information as they process, execute all the information they have processed in a matter of seconds, while 11 potential players on the other side of the ball are trying to disguise themselves from the Quarterback, while trying to rip his head off at the same time. The ball is always in his hands, and he must do his job better than anyone else at all times in order for the team to be successful.

The Quarterback position must put in more time than anyone else. The Quarterback must be the first to arrive and the last to leave—not by seconds, but by minutes to hours. The Quarterback must embrace the fact that he has the most pressure and embrace every challenge the Quarterback position contains. When he performs well and the team wins, he must give the credit to his teammates. If he performs poorly and the team wins, he must give credit to his teammates. When he performs well and the team losses, he must still accept responsibility for the loss.In other words, a Quarterback must have an "I could have done more" mentality at all times. No matter how great he performs, there will always be significant room for improvement. A Quarterback cannot settle for mediocrity; it is a waste of his time and the time of the team. If he wants to be the leader of a football team, he must do everything he can to be the greatest he can be. No matter what level of football you coach or play, my hope is that reading and following this book will assist Quarterbacks on being the greatest player and person they can be on and off the field.

Mindfulness

Before getting into the practice of Mindful Quarterbacking, we must first gain an understanding of what mindfulness is. The most famous definition of mindfulness comes from Dr. Jon Kabat-Zinn: "Mindfulness is paying attention on purpose, in the present moment, and non-judgmentally."

Dr. Kabat-Zinn explains the meaning of his definition: "Attention is the faculty that allows us to navigate our lives in one way or another and to actually know what is happening or to know that we don't know what is happening and find ways to be in a wiser relationship to the things that are going on in our lives, rather than being at the mercy of our own reactions, emotions, crazy thoughts, and fears."

The following outline helps explain mindfulness further:

> Mindfulness has also been described as a state of being present in the here and now—being in the moment, being in your body, not being on autopilot. Mindfulness means owning each moment—good, bad, or ugly. Being grounded is a basic step in the state of being mindful. Mindfulness contributes to a richer, fuller life because you are noticing all the things around you (e.g., not eating an entire meal without tasting it). Mindfulness can help us be calmer. To be mindful, you have to put aside your worries about the future and regrets about the past (at least temporarily). This can be really liberating since much of what upsets us is in other time periods than the present. Being mindful contributes to greater effectiveness in the here and now. If you get all of the worries and regrets out of your mind, it is easier to focus on the things you want to do in the present. (Source: SMART Recovery)

Important Factors in Mindfulness

- Observe with all senses.
- Notice without getting caught up in the activity.
- Participate fully without getting pulled back into worrying.
- One-mindfully (do one thing at a time).
- Be non-reactive. Notice where your mind goes, then pull it back. Don't be upset if your attempts at mindfulness are not perfect.

- Non-judging: Notice your experiences without judging them as positive or negative.
- Describe: Put verbal labels on your experience.
- Not being blinded by emotion and also not being so rational that you ignore your true feelings.

Mindfulness Process

Mindfulness can be applied to sensory experience, thoughts, and emotions by using sustained attention and noticing experiences without reacting. Mindfulness creates space, changing impulsive reactions to thoughtful responses (Figure 1).

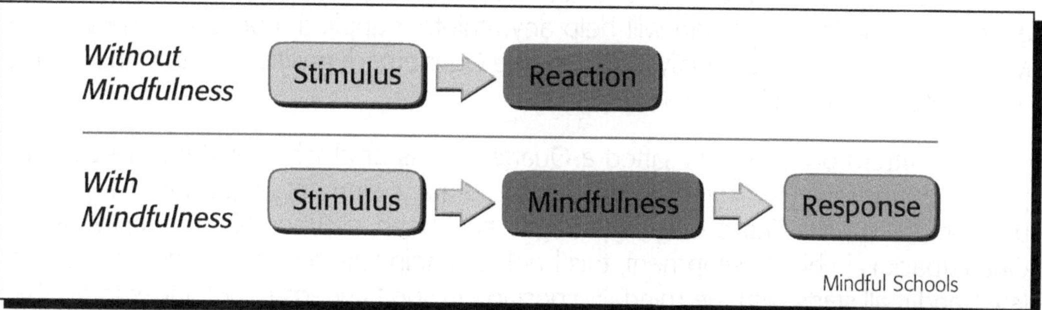

Figure 1

Mindfulschools.org

"We help to grow this space, enabling new, wiser responses that improve attention, learning, emotional regulation, empathy, and conflict resolution.

Introduced into medicine 30 years ago by Dr. Jon Kabat-Zinn, Professor of Medicine Emeritus at the University Of Massachusetts Medical Center, mindfulness has become a successful mainstream influence in medicine, psychology, corporate environments, and now education.

Thirty years of research and (more recently) brain science offers compelling evidence to support the use of mindfulness in education. The application of mindfulness by students and educators has the potential to improve academic achievement, mental health, and inter- and intra-personal relationships."

Mindfulness is a skill that takes time to develop. Like any skill, such as Quarterbacking, it requires a certain level of effort, time, patience, and ongoing practice. Mindfulness can be taught in a number of ways. Mindful Quarterbacking applies the teachings and concepts of mindfulness and applies them into the world and art of Quarterbacking.

Applying Mindfulness With Quarterbacking?

Many athletes have experienced being in the zone at one time or another in their life. When this happens, it always (for most) seems to happen by accident or coincidence.

When we have such a performance, we naturally begin looking for answers on how we can do it all over again. We would even be content just to perform half as well as we just did.

By applying the practice of mindfulness, we can gain tremendous knowledge about our mind, body, and performance while having full awareness of our experiences.

Mindfulness has proven that it can help anyone, in any profession, including athletes. Mindfulness can and will help any athlete if applied. I believe, however, that Mindfulness practice is perfectly suited for the Quarterback position to assist in handling all that the Quarterback position demands.

No matter how physically gifted a Quarterback is or at what level they're currently playing, maximizing the mind is the most important element to playing the greatest position in sports. That's why this book has been written. No matter where a Quarterback is in his development, this book can help take his performance to another level, and it all starts with the mind. No position in sports needs mindfulness more than a Quarterback, and this is why I designed Mindful Quarterbacking.

Book Structure and Purpose

This book is about the mental game of Quarterbacking. I wrote this book with the intention for it to be simple so that any Quarterback or coach at any level can understand and utilize its content. The Quarterback is without question the most important position on the football team—along with the offensive line; never forget them! Without them, the team is nothing; always love them up and show appreciation for how they put their bodies on the line to protect the Quarterback. The sole purpose of this book is to assist the Quarterback in maximizing the mental state of mind so that he can maximize his performance on the field.

I have applied mindfulness throughout the majority of my coaching career and have found it to be very useful and have seen its impact on the young men I have coached, but none more so than the Quarterback position. I have read many great books on Quarterbacking, all of which have been great resources for me throughout my career. However, over the years, I had always wondered why there had never been a book solely dedicated to the mental side of Quarterbacking. A few paragraphs in a few books mention that a Quarterback should be prepared mentally, but providing instructions or solutions for the Quarterback is often overlooked, therefore leaving the Quarterback with a vague understanding on how to maximize the mental side of Quarterbacking. It's not very useful to give demands but then not have the solution. It's similar to asking someone to solve a math equation, but not providing structured steps or a guide to help them solve it. What if your math teacher simply said, "Here's the problem I want you to solve." Then you ask, "How can I solve it?" They reply, "Well, figure it out." That's basically what the vast majority of Quarterbacks hear when it comes to the mental side of Quarterbacking.

I firmly believe that the mental side of Quarterbacking should be structured with the same care and precision as the practice plans, game plans, play calling, progressions, mechanics, and the like. There is the old saying: "I don't want you [Quarterback] to be or play like a robot." That statement is usually only talking about the physical elements of Quarterbacking, and that's because 90 percent of what most Quarterbacks learn is only about the physical part of playing the position. Coaches also want Quarterbacks to just perform, and with that comes another common saying or demand: "Just stop thinking so much." Wouldn't it be beautiful if a Quarterback heard that demand or others similar and had the resources to do just that? Similar to a Quarterback's physical play, it is structured, but coaches still want the Quarterback to perform without thinking about it, hang loose, and use the tools they've been given. The mental side of Quarterbacking needs structure as well as a toolkit to help when some of their circuits start to go haywire or something comes unplugged. Although Quarterbacks are not robots and they should not play like robots, a Quarterback should know how to reboot himself like one, and providing him tools and a manual will help make it much easier.

I do not know everything when it comes to Quarterbacking, nor am I claiming that this book has all of the answers. Like many coaches, I am always learning something new, and I have learned from many other coaches and resources. The Mindful Quarterbacking way isn't the only way, but I do believe it's a very good one. The Quarterback must stay in the present moment mentally, and Mindful Quarterbacking will definitely help him do that. It will also help increase his production on the field.

The purpose of this book is to provide Quarterbacks authentic tools to solve the challenges every Quarterback can face on and off the field, before, during, and after kickoff. In other words, I structured this book to be a playbook for the Quarterback's mind. If this playbook can help even one Quarterback or coach, in even the slightest of ways, I will consider this playbook a success.

This playbook is categorized into several different parts. The foundation of this playbook is structured on the three elements of mindfulness: intention, attention, and attitude. You will read about each of the M-QB principles, how they are grouped (Core Mindfulness Principles, Ps of Preparation, and Cs of Competition) and will also learn how to utilize each of the principles within the three elements of mindfulness.

Each M-QB principle will cover how and why the principle relates to Quarterbacking. As this playbook progresses, there will be "M-QB Situation" readings, where the Quarterback can read about some things that he might encounter (or have previously encountered) as a Quarterback. The Quarterback will then be asked to digest everything he's read, write about how he would usually handle such situations, and also what M-QB principles he can apply to better handle the situation better or differently.

In this playbook, the Quarterback will also be provided meditations, guided imagery exercises, as well as reminders and solutions that he can apply to help maximize focus and always take back the present moment and effectively handle anything that arises throughout their journey.

This playbook will also act as a journal and will have sections where the Quarterback can write, reflect, and evaluate his progress becoming a Mindful Quarterback. In the appendix, there are meditations for pre-practice for each day of the week, goal setting charts, and a weekly/daily reflection log. The appendix will also provide a guide for approaching game time and will provide weekly game time goal setting charts, pre-game meditations, pre-game routine, along with handling in-game situations while in action and on the sideline. The approaching game time area also acts as a journal and will have sections for the Quarterback to write, reflect on, and evaluate his performance as a Mindful Quarterback.

In the extras section of the appendix, you will find M-QB guided imagery as well as ways for the Quarterback to handle dealing with pain and unwelcoming weather conditions.

Before you read about any of the topics touched on, you will first read a few uncategorized subjects which will be useful reminders to take with you during your journey. Something else you will notice about this playbook is that it has limitless combinations to assist you during your journey. Every day and moment is different, and this playbook has unlimited combinations and can always be used and adjusted based on what your needs or intentions are, no matter what arises.

I will truly consider this playbook a success if it can assist just one person in fulfilling their goals and help maximize their potential while playing the greatest and most challenging position in the history of sports.

If you are a coach, I am hopeful that this playbook provides you the tools to help your Quarterbacks succeed on the mental side of playing the position.

If you are a Quarterback reading this playbook, I am hopeful that this playbook will help you achieve better results on the field, as well as off the field.

Quarterbacks can apply the Mindful Quarterbacking way throughout their playing career and in everyday life.

As mentioned earlier, the Mindful Quarterbacking way is not the only way, but I do believe it is a very good one and will help you help any Quarterback at any level reach their fullest potential.

Mindful Quarterbacking Objectives

- To create a Quarterback lifestyle that will allow Quarterbacks to be in the present moment at all times—on and off the field
- To teach the Quarterback to play his position one snap at a time
- To authentically assist the Quarterback in reaching his fullest potential mentally by merging the practice of mindfulness with the skills of Quarterbacking.
- To be a reliable and productive resource for all Quarterbacks and coaches at all levels and to assist them in maximizing the art of Quarterbacking
- To coach the Quarterback on how to compete in a very calm and focused manner.
- To teach the Quarterback how to practice, lead, and compete within the confines of his authentic self.
- To teach the Quarterback to maximize his focus.
- To teach Quarterbacks how to become proactive and productive leaders on and off the field.
- To provide the Quarterback with tools that can be used to maximize performance on the field of play and in everyday life.
- To authentically teach the Quarterback to be in the present moment at all times, which will allow him to be coached at an optimal level and in turn take his performance to an optimal level.
- To authentically enhance the Quarterback's positive state of mind and provide tools that will give him confidence to handle all distractions and obstacles that comes his way in a positive and productive manner on and off the field.
- To assist the Quarterback in troubleshooting mental and physical barriers.
- To provide the Quarterback with assistance in goal-setting and decision-making.
- To authentically teach the Quarterback productive ways to handle emotions, pressure, adversity, and unwelcoming weather conditions.
- To provide drills that will assist the Quarterback in maximizing his performance during practice, pre-game, and game time.
- To be a lifelong resource, mentor, life coach, and Quarterback coach to all Quarterbacks.

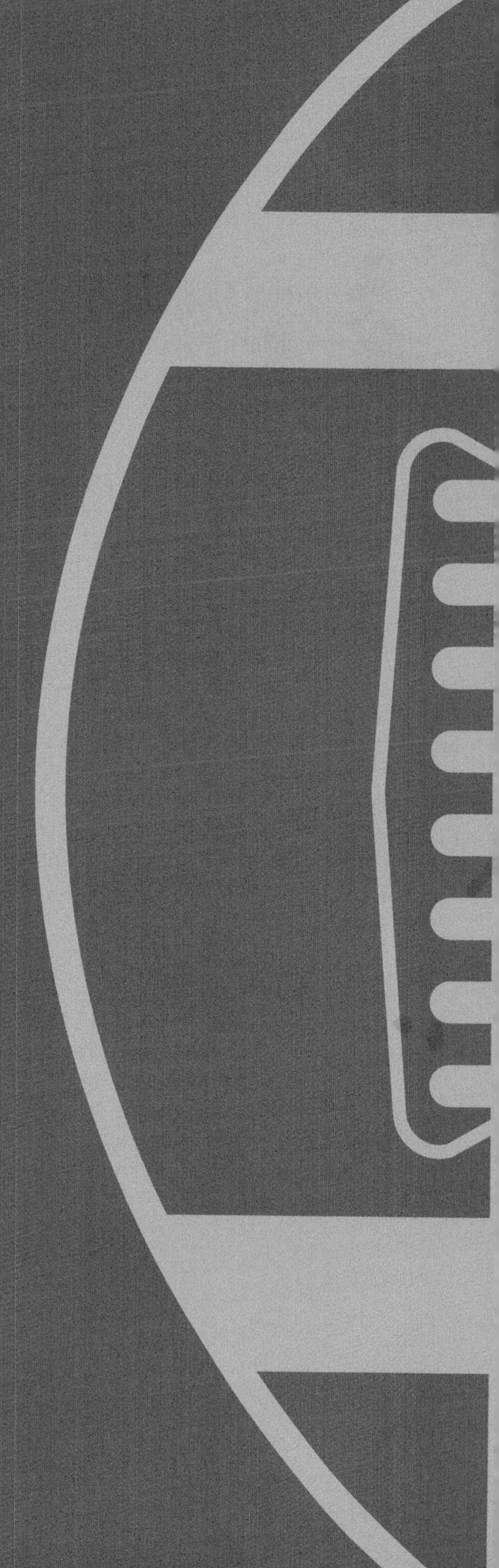

CHAPTER 1
Hakuna Matata

Hakuna Matata: what a wonderful phrase. Odds are that every reader of this playbook knows that Hakuna Matata means "no worries" and comes from the legendary movie *The Lion King*. If you have not yet seen *The Lion King*, set this playbook down and watch the film and return to reading after you have seen the film. The phrase Hakuna Matata is a major part of Mindful Quarterbacking. The first question you might be asking yourself is, "How does Hakuna Matata apply to playing the Quarterback position or even mindfulness?" Several examples from the film relate very well to everyday life and playing the Quarterback position. Also, many of the lessons presented in the film are directly related to some of the principles associated with mindfulness.

Hakuna Matata is a phrase that tells us not to worry, but what does worry mean? To worry is to think about problems and/or fears that we think *could* happen (i.e., have not happened yet) and taking those thoughts and forming them into our mind as realities. Worry can also impact our entire attitude and approach to Quarterbacking or everyday life, because what we believe often becomes our reality. Worrying is pointless. Worrying is the equivalent to walking around throughout your life dragging a boat with you and wearing a lifejacket waiting for a flashflood to happen. There is no need for the boat or lifejacket (worry) and carrying that extra weight around waiting for something awful or bad to happen. In terms of Quarterbacking, it is equivalent to preparing a list of apologies and excuses to present for playing poorly on game day when the game hasn't even started yet. It slows us down physically and most importantly, it wears us down mentally, which will have a negative impact on performance. Worrying is an activity developed out of habit; most people who worry too much do so because it's become a part of their nature, and this could happen for a multitude of reasons throughout a person's life. Thankfully, for every problem there is a solution, and applying mindfulness practice will help the Quarterback obtain and maintain attention on and toward the present moment.

There's an awesome scene in *The Lion King* where Rafiki randomly hits Simba on the head with his bamboo stick. Simba asks why Rafiki did that to him. Rafiki replies, "It doesn't matter. It's in the past." In which Simba replies, "Yeah, but it still hurts." Rafiki then proceeds to tell Simba, "Yes, the past can hurt, but the way I see it, you can either run from it or learn from it." Rafiki then swings his bamboo stick at Simba's head again; this time, Simba dodges the stick and takes it away from Rafiki. Rafiki is pleased to see Simba learned the lesson, a lesson which motivates Simba to move forward in life.

Hakuna Matata does not mean we shouldn't worry about anything at all and just let things happen as they may and not worry about the consequences. Hakuna Matata means to bring our mind and attention to all of the things we can control and to live in the present moment. Doing so brings so much more joy and happiness. Hakuna Matata is also about not judging ourselves: "No worries, no one is perfect, move forward, it's going to be just fine and I'll come back stronger." Hakuna Matata can also remind us to let things go that have already passed and to understand that life will continue (Circle of Life) and better times are ahead, no matter how unfortunate or great the past might have been. Even when negative things do happen in life or on the field of play, Hakuna Matata: we'll be prepared!

CHAPTER 2
Controllable Goals

Everyone has been asked the question: "What are your goals?" More often than not, we have more than one goal and list off a bunch of the different goals and when we want to obtain them. As we present our thoughts on what we want to accomplish, the next question we are asked is often one that causes hesitation or stumps us: "How do you plan to accomplish those goals?" After a few seconds of deep thinking, we quickly rattle off a few things or steps we will take. Oftentimes, we don't truly have a complete answer to what step we will take to accomplish our goals, but we answer the question to avoid embarrassment for not having a well-thought-out plan or because we feel as if we are being challenged by the person questioning us. Forming goals in our mind is the first step toward achieving our goals. It's very healthy and important that we see what it is we want to accomplish along with the romanticism of it all. Although forming goals in our mind is the first step toward achieving our goals, actually accomplishing the goals is the final step, and there are a few steps in between forming our goals and accomplishing our goals. If you at this moment have formed a goal in your mind, congratulations; you're already heading in the right direction.

The question "How do you plan to accomplish those goals?" is a very broad question and might be impossible to answer in full detail (even if we have a plan) because we simply might not have the time to explain everything, and we simply might not want to go into detail about the steps we're going to take. Maybe we're simply protective of the road we're taking and don't want anyone creating traffic. The best answer we can give and the way in which this playbook will teach is: "Just one moment at a time." We only have control over our goals by working in the present moment. Our goals do not move away, so we need to just relax and allow each moment to take us there. No matter what our goals and expectations might be (long-term or short-term), we only have control over them by doing what can be done in the present. Maximizing every present moment should become the ultimate goal because it's the best way toward achieving the ultimate goal.

Quarterback Exercise: Write down six goals you want to accomplish this year.

1.
2.
3.
4.
5.
6.

Now it's time for a small reality check. The two questions addressed are: "What are your goals?" and "How do you plan to accomplish those goals?" The keywords in each of these questions are *you* and *your*. Too often, people set goals over which they have no control. When I ask any Quarterback I've worked with to write down a list of goals they want to accomplish, many of them are goals they cannot control because they involve so many other people and factors.

Some common answers include:

1. Win the championship.
2. Make it to the playoffs.
3. Become a better leader.
4. Throw for 4,000 yards.
5. Be more focused.
6. Watch more film.

The reality is Quarterbacks do not have complete control over numbers 1, 2, and 4.

Numbers 1 and 2: Winning a championship or making it to the playoffs takes a complete team effort from players, coaches, scouts, film crew, administration, team trainers, and team doctors, and is also impacted by any number of other factors, such as the number of injuries, the ability of the opponents, the playing schedule, weather, and so forth.

Number 4: The Quarterback can throw the most beautiful pass anyone on this planet has ever seen, but he cannot control if the receiver catches or drops the football. He also cannot necessarily stop a defender from making a spectacular play on the football, just like he cannot always stop a perfectly thrown back shoulder pass. The Quarterback and his teammates are an extension of one another. Wide receivers might have goals of having 1,000 receiving yards and 20 touchdowns, but they are not in control of how the Quarterback throws, when he throws, the coverage, the pass protection, or the play calling. Stats are for people who are in it for themselves.

The reality is that the Quarterback has complete control over numbers 3, 5, and 6.

Number 3: Becoming a better leader is absolutely something the Quarterback is in complete control over, and it's something he can work on and evaluate every single day. The Quarterback becoming a better leader may not guarantee wins and championships, but it does increase the team's chances of winning and going in the right direction. It can only help!

Who knows, maybe the Quarterback becoming a better leader will motivate the other players to go the extra mile for him and the team. Perhaps they'll make that big catch or fight to pick up that extra defender, and perhaps the coach will trust the ball being in the Quarterback's hands more often. Not guaranteed, but the Quarterback becoming a better leader can only help the odds.

Numbers 5 and 6: Focus is a cornerstone of how well an athlete will perform. Improving focus is going to assist in every area of Quarterbacking—on and off the field. The more focused the Quarterback becomes and the more he studies (watching more film), the more information he will absorb and the better he will perform for the team.

Tom Brady was once asked in an interview about what his goals were for the upcoming season, and he mentioned that his goal is to make sure that every single day and at the start of every single season he prepares himself to give his team the greatest chance of winning by preparing himself the best way he possibly can in every area and always finding ways to get better each and every day for his team, and that has been and always will be the goal. This statement followed through with actions has propelled Brady to become one of the greatest Quarterbacks in the history of the game—some people even regard him as the greatest Quarterback of all time. His craft is built around being the best he possibly can for his team and controlling what he can control and also displaying a great deal of selflessness.

Although this playbook cannot guarantee a Quarterback will have a career such as Tom Brady's, it will help him learn to maximize what a Quarterback can control, which will help a team's chances of being successful. That's what the Quarterback position and the game of football is all about.

CHAPTER 3

Ego-Self vs. Auto-Self

The ego or "ego-self" is what distracts us from being able to "just do it." For example, how many times have you seen a Quarterback throw an incomplete pass to a wide-open receiver or just having an off day completing passes? It gets much more frustrating when he's been throwing a particular route or pattern just fine before, and all of a sudden he just can't seem to do anything right. He begins to get upset with himself, and his ego begins to sneak into his mind and tells him things such as, "I'm not good enough!" "What is wrong with me?" or "How did I miss that throw?" What he does next is naturally what most people believe they should do, and that is to try harder and that is when he begins to give himself demands on what he should be doing to correct whatever the problem is, and begins talking to himself and saying, "Stop dropping your elbow!" "Keep your eyes upfield!" "Stop squeezing the ball so tight!" "Set your feet!" and many more demands. Trying harder is not the solution; rather, it becomes the biggest problem.

You're now asking yourself: "How can a Quarterback trying harder be a problem?" The answer: he already knows how to throw a football, has been coached on how to throw a football, or has simply thrown a football his entire life. Something I teach and advise the Quarterback to do is to simply allow the natural progression of throwing the football to naturally come back. This can be done by a Quarterback simply being kind to himself and remembering that he has not forgotten how to throw; he simply has things in his mind that need to be removed so he can get back to doing things the way he already knows how to do them and has been coached to do them no matter what it might be.

When it comes to throwing, instead of a Quarterback going through his mind trying to remember how to fix every mechanical problem possible, he should take a deep breath and take his mind to when he was simply throwing out in the backyard with friends. A Quarterback should remember how he would just let the ball fly and how beautiful that spiral in the air looked. A Quarterback should remember the soft feeling of the leather of the ball as it came out of his hands and the nice "whip" or "whoosh" sound it made as it left his hands. He should remember how effortless it was. It was simply joyful, and throwing the ball well was simply automatic. What a Quarterback is experiencing during those times is what I like to call the auto-self. I use the term "auto-self" because it has helped my Quarterbacks best remember to let their physical performance happen "automatically" and not interrupt it with their ego. The core foundation of the ego-self versus the auto-self of Mindful Quarterbacking was adopted from W. Timothy Gallwey's famous book *The Inner Game of Tennis*.

The auto-self is what we already do, what we know how to do, what happens naturally and without us necessarily having to think about it at all. In order for the auto-self to be able to function fully, we must quiet the ego-self. The auto-self is something we should be mindful of, but we don't give it much thought. When we are mindful of things, we auto-correct and are still in motion, allowing the other parts to stay connected. It is like breathing. We do not have to think to breathe; it happens on its own. We are aware we are breathing, but we do not concentrate to make sure it is happening; we trust it, and therefore we can always work in the moment.

When the ego-self becomes in charge, our entire being becomes tight and defensive and is equivalent to going into a panic attack, trying to catch our breath. When people go into a panic attack or are startled in some capacity, they are told to simply calm down and breathe, and all they have to do is remember and it naturally comes back to them, just like throwing a football or any other part of Quarterbacking.

M-QB Solution

- Don't overadjust.
- Remember that you remember.
- Be kind to yourself.
- Be aware of your breathing.
- Allow the auto-self to do its job.

CHAPTER 4

It's a Game—Very Serious Fun

Just in case you have forgotten, football is a game. Football should be and is often taken seriously all over the country from youth flag football to the National Football League. However, many players from youth to the National Football League seem to forget why they are playing the game. Although the game needs to be taken seriously, and the Quarterback position is the most important position on the team, many players struggle because they forget their love for the game and really do take it too seriously.

It's scientifically proven that when someone enjoys what they do, they perform far superior to those who do not. Those who remember why they play football or fell in love with the game perform better than most. A player who loves the game runs on to the practice field fired up, he runs around trying to pump up his teammates, talks about how beautiful the day is even if it's pouring down rain and the field is nothing but mud. What does this do? It sets the tone for him and hopefully the rest of the team.

Displaying enthusiasm can also help relax the mind so when it's time to flip the switch and bring attention to the task at hand, the player is only thinking about the game and what he needs to do to play the game effectively. When displaying enthusiasm, players are not thinking about the pressure of losing, messing up, consequences, fans, media, what-ifs, and such. All they care about is the love for the game. If they love the game, they will enjoy the process and give the game their greatest efforts.

Like any relationship in life, there will be rough times, heartbreaking times, and times where we just want to quit, but as long as we remember why we love the person and put that first, it will remind us of the great times and motivate us to get through it all and continue. A Quarterback's relationship with the game of football should be no different. He should remember the love for the game, and play the game with passion and with joy. A Quarterback should give back to the game by giving his greatest efforts in preparation and play and by being fully present in the experience. If a Quarterback does those things, there will be no regrets. Football should be all about very serious fun.

Quarterback Exercise: Write down 10 reasons you love the game of football and/or playing the Quarterback position. Take as much time as you need, even if you need a few hours or a few days, and come back to fill in your responses. Give this exercise sincere thought. Always come back to this page to remind yourself of why you love the game and the Quarterback position.

Why do I love playing football and/or playing the Quarterback position?

1.
2.
3.
4.
5.
6.
7.
8.
9.
10.

CHAPTER 5
Mindful Quarterbacking Principles

M-QB Principles

As you gain more knowledge about the M-QB principles, you discover that the M-QB principles are interchangeable within each of the three elements of mindfulness (intention, attention, attitude), something that will be covered later in this playbook. All of these principles relate to Quarterbacking as well as mindfulness. Take a look at the M-QB principles in the wordbank in Table 5-1. Your first impression might be that there is no structure. When I first designed Mindful Quarterbacking and established the M-QB principles, this is basically what it looked like: a bunch of principles that were effective and useful, but that lacked structure and that, if structured, would give Quarterbacks a much more impactful way to apply the principles.

Communication	Trust	Control	Awareness	Patience	Confidence
Perseverance	Calmness	Present Moment	Breathing	Coachable	Beginner's Mind
Compassion	Passion	Non-Judging	Competitive	Selflessness	Pride
	Authentic Self	Courage	Self-Observation	Consistency	

Table 5-1. M-QB Principles

To better structure the M-QB principles, they are grouped into three categories that can be used interchangeably within the three elements:

- Core mindfulness principles
- Ps of preparation
- Cs of competition

M-QB Principles by Category

Communication	Trust	Control	Awareness	Patience	Confidence
Perseverance	Calmness	Present Moment	Breathing	Coachable	Beginner's Mind
Compassion	Passion	Non-Judging	Competitive	Selflessness	Pride
	Authentic Self	Courage	Self-Observation	Consistency	

Table 5-2

Although "present moment" will be categorized and presented under the core mindfulness principles, it is also the most universal principle and applies to all three of the categories. The blank boxes in the chart are for you to fill in your own intention/attention/attitude term or goal. "It's all about the now."

CHAPTER 6

The Core Principles of Mindfulness

Present Moment

"We have only now, only this single eternal moment opening and unfolding before us, day and night."

—Jack Kornfield

The present moment or "the now" is the period of time between the past and the future. The present moment is the only moment, and it's the only moment in which we can truly experience and operate. The present can be maximized, or it can be used for dwelling on things that will serve no purpose. The present moment is the greatest gift we can be given because it's only within this moment that we grow and discover. When we are fully in the present, the thoughts of the past are removed and thoughts of the future expectations are non-existent, and if and when thoughts of the past or future do arrive, we simply allow those thoughts to pass without clinging to them emotionally.

The present moment is all about the current down and distance, the current rep, the current exchange from center, the current handoff, the current pass. The next moment will become the present moment when it arrives and the past moments are gone forever. As a Quarterback, living in the present is the single-most important area of playing the position no matter how badly or how well things are going on or off the field. Practicing being present will help the Quarterback maximize his potential and will help remove all thoughts from the past and worries about the future.

When we work only in the present, it begins to spread into our lives at home, school, and in the huddle. How many times have you heard a Quarterback say, "I'm thinking too much!"? He begins to get angry with himself because he wants to stop thinking and just play, but he is worried what a coach is thinking and what his teammates, family, friends, girlfriend, and media are all thinking. He begins to wish he could go back and fix the mistakes he's just made or starts hoping to finish well to avoid criticism. All of those things the Quarterback is thinking about and trying to correct are gone or out of reach at the moment. The greatest way to correct anything is to live in the space of time between the past and the future.

Something to remember is: even when we are in the present moment, things from the past and thoughts of the future will arise, but if we remember to pull our minds back to the present moment, we are being mindful and winning the moment. Something else we can do is: when something does arise, just notice it and allow it to pass naturally without feeding it and work to have the presence of mind or intention to stay in the present. It takes time, just remember that it's a practice, and the sooner we begin, the better we become. We have all experienced being fully engaged in the present moment in many parts of our life, and may have also experienced it on the football field as well.

M-QB Solution

- It's all about the now.
- Allow the past to fade away.
- Bring your attention to what is in front of you now.
- When thoughts of the past arrive, don't cling to them emotionally.
- The greatest way to correct anything is to live in the present.

Beginner's Mind

> *"If your mind is empty, it is always ready for anything, it is open to everything. In the beginner's mind, there are many possibilities, but in the expert's mind, there are few."*
>
> —Shunryu Suzuki

Developing a beginner's mind is an important skill for a Quarterback to practice in order for him to unlock his full potential. So often, Quarterbacks believe or act as if they have it all figured out and cannot allow themselves to learn something new or even absorb the information they already know and understand without allowing their ego to get in the way and say outwardly or internally, "I know this stuff already. Why do we keep doing it?" Or saying, "I know, I know" with frustration and shaking their head.

The beginner's mind is about observing the present moment as if it is brand new or a new beginning no matter what has happened in the past or what knowledge we currently have about any particular thing. A player who practices with a beginner's mind finds fulfillment in everything they are learning or repeating and understands that no matter how similar something might be, it is in fact completely different because it is now a new moment. Nothing is ever exactly the same, so why not treat it as a new event? During practice, a Quarterback might be asked to run the same play over and over and over again. Although the play is the same, the events surrounding the play are not. The Quarterback and the team become tired and sweaty, substitutions happen, mistakes happen, and improvements happen. A mindful Quarterback will approach everything with a beginner's mind. This does not mean the Quarterback forgets everything that he knows or act as if he know nothing; it means to see every moment (every snap) as a new experience and with a somewhat rookie state of mind by absorbing everything within each moment and not hindering himself by being an expert of knowledge all the time. A Quarterback might very well be an expert at a particular aspect of Quarterbacking or anywhere in life, but if he keeps a beginner's mind, even as an expert, the worst that can happen is that he improves what he already knows so well.

If we keep an expert mind or ego throughout our life on and off the field, it will carry over into what is called arrogance when it's time to learn something new. The expert mind will become so filled with ego that making mistakes or learning something new becomes difficult to handle, and the mind closes because we already "know everything." When we keep a beginner's mind, we find more joy in learning, and when it's time to learn something we've never learned before, we will better absorb that information and will find joy and fulfillment in the process. The beginner's mind allows the Quarterback to absorb more information, become more coachable, vanquish the ego-self, and help him with present moment awareness. Just remember that the problem with knowing everything is that a person will never have the joyful experience of learning something new. With a beginner's mind, every day and every event is a new adventure, and the way we approach it sets the tone for the outcome.

M-QB Solution

- Let go of being an expert.
- Give all information your full care and attention (repetitive or new).
- Remember nothing is ever exactly the same.
- Remember that your ego is trying to prevent you from learning; let it go.
- Treat every moment as a new adventure.
- You can always learn something new.

Breathing

"To meditate with mindful breathing is to bring body and mind back to the present moment so that you do not miss your appointment with life."

—Thích Nhát Hanh

Breathing is the foundation to living. Breathing happens automatically, and because we do not have to think to breathe, we often forget to maximize our breathing throughout everyday life. If the ability to breathe is the foundation or reason why we live and we cannot live without it, it should be the something that we try to maximize and make stronger. The importance of maximizing our breathing is just as, if not more, important than maximizing our physical bodies to become bigger, faster, stronger. We can live without bulging muscles and running fast as lighting, but we cannot live without the ability to breathe, and breathing can be developed or improved, just as the physical body can.

How often have you been told throughout your life on or off the field to "just breathe"? It is natural for us to take for granted things that happen automatically for us and that we just trust to work. There is an old saying that if a person had to think to breathe, they would die because the mind is so preoccupied with things of this world. A Quarterback practicing breathing techniques is going to assist himself in stabilizing his thoughts and emotions, bringing him back to the present moment or simply keeping him there. As mentioned previously, football is an emotional game. There are going to be times where a Quarterback feels that everything seems to be spiraling out of control or times where he can't really get into a groove. For example, say a Quarterback is in a highly competitive, low scoring contest, he cannot run the ball, and to top it all off the offensive line is getting destroyed when he is dropping back to pass or just not clicking that day. He is getting placed on his butt every other snap whether it's by taking a big shot, getting knocked down, or being sacked. Frustration sets in naturally because he and everyone in the stadium know one score can possibly win the game, but again, he cannot find a groove.

As frustration sets in, his emotions go haywire, and when this happens, his breathing becomes short, rapid, out-of-control, or flat out stops. Without him knowing it (because of lack of observing), the muscles in his body begin to tense up, causing him to have lack of movement when needing to throw, and he loses power, velocity, and mobility. He also begins to communicate less effectively and loses the ability to slow down his thinking, and everything he knows begins to go out the window. He begins to forget the simplest of things, such as where to open up on a basic handoff. Frustration also causes him to give into his emotions and to want to speed things up and "show the situation who's boss," but that will never work long-term and will only hurt the situation because the situation is still controlling him, not the other way around.

One of the major pieces of advice to take into account is: a Quarterback should never signal for the snap until he is mentally ready to run the next play. Some systems and game situations will require him to snap the ball much faster, but by making breathing a part of his everyday practice on the field, he and his breathing practice will naturally adapt, and he will always be mentally ready for the next snap. Practicing breathing will allow the Quarterback to slow down his thoughts, come back to "the now," remain in command of his physical body and abilities, stay loose, and communicate more clearly and effectively. Most importantly, it will help maximize the team's chances of being successful.

M-QB Solution

- Practice breathing intentionally every day.
- The importance of practicing breathing is just as important as lifting weights.
- Practicing breathing will help stabilize your thoughts and emotions.
- Identify when frustration sets in and utilize breathing practice.
- Remember that breathing will help your body stay relaxed so you can better perform.
- Never take a snap until your mind is clear.

Trust

"A bird sitting on a tree is never afraid of the branch breaking, because its trust is not on the branch but on its own wings. Always believe in yourself."

—Unknown

"I trust you" is one of the most powerful statements in the human language. Without trust, nothing can be accomplished. At one point or another, a Quarterback might have said or will say, "I trust you!" Hearing those words oftentimes boosts a player's confidence and enthusiasm to go get the job done. Although coaches might trust a player, having true trust in himself is most important. If a player doesn't trust himself, why would anyone else trust or believe in him? A Quarterback must have trust in all of the work he has put in to enhance his skills, just as he needs to have trust in the game plan put into place by the coaches.

The first step for a Quarterback learning how to trust himself is identifying his areas or strengths and areas he needs to improve. One of the biggest disconnects is a Quarterback not exactly knowing what his strengths and areas that need improvement are. Maybe he throws the short to intermediate passing game very well, but struggles with the deep ball or having the patience to sell the play-action pass. Some Quarterbacks are too afraid to admit there are areas they need to improve and, instead of striving to improve them, they will try to sweep it under the rug hoping and praying that there will not be a situation that arises where they are called to do something with which they are not comfortable. He has trust in himself with the short to intermediate pass plays, but when a play-action pass is called, he begins second guess his abilities. When he takes the snap and turns to deliver the run-action to the running back, and he doesn't trust himself or those around him, his mind begins to think, "I'm about to get hit!" and he rushes the process. The first problem is taking a snap before being mentally prepared. The second problem is anticipating future outcomes over which he has no control over. The third problem is lacking trust in teammates and coaches. The last problem is that he is only making the lack of trust worse by not executing the play exactly the way it is designed, therefore losing the trust of the coaches and teammates and also giving the advantage to the defense.

A good place for a Quarterback to start developing trust is communicating with the coach what they both see as his areas as strengths and devising a plan that will utilize those strengths are much as possible. There will be times where areas that the Quarterback is working to improve are going to be needed, and it will take a combination of trust and courage when those times arrive, because they will arrive. When people trust each other to do their job, the game is so much smoother and enjoyable. Following are three very basic steps for the Quarterback to follow before taking a snap:

- Receive the play.
- Identify the situation.
- Execute as planned.

Following those three steps will help the Quarterback remember to have:

- If he has communicated with the coach about the play calls that week, then he can trust the call.
- When he studies as he should, he will trust what he is seeing.
- The Quarterback knows that he can trust his execution because the play call is set up as best as possible for the situation he is facing, therefore allowing him to play freely, thoroughly, without worry, and trusting the outcome will be favorable.

M-QB Solution

- Trust yourself.
- Know your strengths.
- Know the areas you need to improve.
- Prepare with purpose.

Quarterback Exercise:

1. What do you believe are your greatest strengths as a Quarterback?

2. Why are those areas your strengths?

3. What do you believe are the areas you need to improve as a Quarterback?

4. How do you plan to go about improving those areas?

Self-Observation

> *"The most fundamental aggression to ourselves, the most fundamental harm we can do to ourselves, is to remain ignorant by not having the courage and the respect to look at ourselves honestly and gently."*
>
> —Pema Chödrön

The Quarterback position is played with the eyes, mind, and heart. A Quarterback's ability to see the field is important, it is also important for him to observe what is going on within himself. A Quarterback puts so much time, effort, and energy into what the defense is doing or what is going on around him (which are good things), but he can often forget to observe himself and how he is impacting his own performance. Football is an emotional game, and more often than not, a Quarterback will wear his emotions on his sleeve for better or worse. In situations where things are not going his way, body-language and attitude are impacted because of what enters his mind, and he can often act out what enters his mind. The Quarterback throws an interception, his mind gets upset, and then his body displays being upset, such as dropping his head, screaming, slapping his hands together in disappointment, gritting his teeth, clinching his fist, placing his hands on his head, or slapping his helmet, calling himself all kinds of names or insults. Though some of those things can be viewed as stress relief to some, it's actually creating more stress and tension both mentally and physically.

Everything we do with our bodies sends a signal to our brains, and the brain reacts accordingly. When a Quarterback does some of the actions described, it creates mental, muscular, and environmental tension. He begins to perform out of frustration and desperation, and the environment around him spirals out of control. He is no longer playing with his auto-self; he is playing with the ego-self and to the tune of the environment. Coaches in the past have probably spoken to him about the importance of having good body language no matter what the situation might be. This does not mean the Quarterback must stop being competitive or that he cannot show any emotion, but he should be mindful of what he is displaying and what everyone else is seeing from him. When he begins to feel the ego-self kick in after a mistake, he should take a moment to observe the emotions that arise rather than react to the emotions that arise. Body language sets the tone for the present moment for everyone else involved, most importantly for himself.

M-QB Solution

- When things go wrong, pay attention to what thoughts enter your mind.
- Be mindful and observant of your body language.
- Remember that everything you do sends a signal to your brain, and your brain reacts accordingly.
- Work on not displaying negative body language because it creates tension in the body and also tension in the environment. Your body language can impact the belief others have in you.

Awareness

"We practice mindfulness by maintaining a moment-by-moment awareness of our thoughts, feelings, bodily sensations, and the surrounding environment."

—Melli O'Brien

The part of awareness discussed in this section is about in the external environment surrounding the Quarterback and giving it full Attention with nothing else in his vision or on his mind. The most valuable weapon the Quarterback carries is not his arm or mobility; it's his eyes. The reason the eyes are most vital is that they train the brain, and the brain trains the body how to respond to what we see. The Quarterback must play the position with his eyes up and be aware of everything that is happening on the field. Increasing awareness will allow him to better identify the situation and execute. He must observe the field with full intention and with purpose and observe with soft eyes. Giving full attention to the play call brought into the huddle or signaled from the sideline, making sure his teammates are aligned in the proper formation, making sure the offensive line has the correct information, identifying the defensive front, secondary, the defense's pre-snap movement with or without motion are all a few aspects of the game that require awareness.

Increasing awareness will assist the Quarterback to trust what he is seeing, not what his imagination sees or what his mind tells him to see, but just seeing things for what they are and executing according to what he sees and how he's been coached to execute. I have heard Quarterbacks from the youth level to the pro levels say, "I didn't see him" when they've thrown an interception, or "I should have seen that," and my favorite, "Where did he come from?" Lack of awareness might be the reason one of the wide receivers marches over to the Quarterback upset because he was "wide open," and although sometimes they are wrong about being so wide open, they could very well be right, and the Quarterback wants to decrease the chance of missing those types of opportunities.

A Quarterback's coaches have probably said to him at some point, either in a practice or a game, "You need to pay more attention and be aware of what's going on." Taking the time and care to prepare will decrease the chances of making mistakes, but oftentimes the simple mistakes come from a quick lapse of awareness in the present moment. Outside of just knowing the X's and O's and everything on film, it's important that the Quarterback works on increasing everything that he sees by training his eyes to see the field (refer to Appendix A-2). Even when mistakes are made, he will be able to answer these questions quicker and much more effectively; he will know how to correct it because he will be aware of the mistake he made, not lost searching for answers. He will also be able to see the game within the game better. As a Quarterback, the more aware he is, the better chance the team has of succeeding.

M-QB Solution

- Observe the field with full purpose and observe with soft eyes.
- Train your eyes to see the field. Your eyes are your most valuable weapon.
- Remember, your eyes train the brain, and the brain trains your body how to respond.

Selflessness

"The grass is greener where you water it."

—Neil Barringham

Being selfless is one of the most important qualities in the world. Being selfless means that a person performs good deeds without seeking acknowledgment or praise of any kind. Being selfless is a skill or action that comes from the heart and is often one of the most rewarding feelings a person can obtain. Performing a selfless act can create a contagious environment of selflessness because the people we are assisting also identify those actions as selfless. An example of a selfless act as a Quarterback would be seeking out one of his teammates, such as the backup quarterback. He and the backup are competing every single day. He notices that the backup is struggling with the system in practice and in the film room. The coach is on his back every second of every day, and the pressure is really getting to him. He can see that the backup is giving a great effort and wants to do well, but something seems to be genuinely wrong, or he just needs some help. A selfless Quarterback will seek to help the backup by pulling him aside when no one is around or giving him a call and offering to assist him in every way he can. No one on the team or the coaches know that he is doing this for him, and the Quarterback is doing it because he genuinely cares about the well-being of his teammate and wanting to see him be successful. When the backup starts performing better, someone who is selfless does not seek the attention for the improvement; he simply observes, smiles, and feels inner gratification and also very happy for the person he helped. He sacrifices his ego for the betterment of others. Of course, the better he gets, the tougher the competition, but that is not what is on the Quarterback's mind. A Mindful Quarterback does everything he can for others first, while remaining focused on maximizing his own abilities.

Another example of a selfless act would be taking extra time before or after practice to go through the playbook or routes with a wide receiver who is struggling. The Quarterback is simply out there to help the wide receiver become a better player. He is not thinking about everyone standing out there watching him help his teammate, hoping to get attention and being told "That's nice of you" or "Good job." When someone performs a selfless act, he is simply in the present moment of the action, with pure intentions. Selflessness helps build camaraderie and trust between others because it creates a culture of sincerity and trust. Selflessness is a skill that becomes easier the more we practice. It is very natural for the ego to chime in and want to take credit for selfless deeds. When the ego begins to chime in, simply allow it to say what it has to say and remind us of the purpose of selflessness, and after a while, the ego begins to struggle more and more to influence us to speak up about what we've done for others or seek attention. It's all about intentions before and during deeds and how we conduct ourselves after deeds. Practicing performing selfless actions is going to help us grow as a person and will be some of the most intrinsically rewarding moments of our lives off and on the field.

M-QB Solution

- Look to perform at least one simple selfless act once a week, on or off the field.
- Do not seek attention for performing good deeds.
- Sacrifice your ego for the betterment of others.
- Have genuine care about the well-being and success of your teammates.

Non-Judging

> *"If you were your own jury at your own trial, I'd be really worried about you."*
>
> —Mindful Quarterbacking

Being non-judgmental is a skill that takes time to develop. Whether we know it or not, we are constantly judging ourselves, others, or the world around us. You might have been told at one point in your life to not pass judgment on others, but what about also not judging yourself? It is no secret that we are our harshest critics and can often judge ourselves harder than anyone else can. Judgment is ingrained in us since birth. Everything in the world around us (especially the Western world) is labeled as good, bad, like, dislike, win, loss, right, wrong, smart, dumb, pass, and fail. Now, being judgmental is not going to go away, but we can improve our awareness of how judgmental we are while not coming down on ourselves within those judgments.

A simple example would be a Quarterback calling the wrong play in the huddle and as he heads to the sideline, the coach is irate that he mistakenly called the wrong play that ended badly. Oftentimes, a Quarterback will instantly look at and feel what is unfolding and apply judgment and say things like, "I'm an idiot" or "How can I be so dumb?" At moments like this, he is absorbing the anger from the coach and a mishap and applying them to his entire being. A Mindful Quarterback will observe everything in its totality, identify the problem, and only judge the events for what they are. The Quarterback should tell himself, "I made a mistake, and I will pay more attention the next time" or "I just need to relax and understand that mistakes happen, and this is not who I am. This is a single event that took place not long ago, and I have to move forward."

It's important that we learn from experiences when our minds begin to wander and not be judgmental of the experience in a way that will keep us from living in the present moment and seeing events for what they truly are. When we judge things that arise, our minds develop a false or incomplete picture of what is actually there or happening. There is an expression I've often heard some of my players say when certain events arrive: "It is what it is." That is a very true statement, but often utilized when someone is highly emotional and does not want to see things for what they are. When we refocus our attention and become aware of everything around us and observe emotions, we can truly and genuinely see that "It is what it is" in a non-judgmental way. Being non-judgmental does not mean we stop caring, evaluating, or improving. A Quarterback is not going to call the wrong play in the huddle and just walk back as if nothing happened, but he will not be judgmental of himself and attach the labels he says to himself to his entire being.

When a Quarterback practices being non-judgmental with himself, he will see how it impacts his communication with coaches and teammates and improves his qualities as a leader. He should always remember that everything that goes on in his mind is 99.99 percent of the time bigger and harsher than what is actually going on. Once he removes those judgments from his mind, he can simply say, "Hakuna Matata, I've got this. I've learned, and everything is going to be alright" and get ready for the next snap.

M-QB Solution

- Only judge or identify the events for what they truly are in their totality.
- Being judgmental will keep you from living in the present moment.
- Remember that people are human, mistakes happen, and move on. It does no good dwelling on mistakes.

Authentic Self

"Authenticity is the daily practice of letting go of who we think we're supposed to be and embracing who we are."

—Brene Brown

Authentic self can be defined as: the true you; aligned and congruent self-image, stature, values, beliefs, goals, behavior, word, and public image (Emotional Competency). Every single one of us is born authentic. However, as we grow, we begin to form to what society expects us to be and are taught to live up to certain expectations and be or conduct ourselves a certain way. Being our authentic selves is a practice. Far too often as people, we try to be someone or something we are not to try to gain public approval, praise, and appreciation. When we begin to seek approval from others and meet their expectations, we often lose our self-esteem and begin to feel fake or artificial and begin to lose our identity, so we begin to live life being someone we are not, which is no way to live. This is not to say that we cannot learn from watching others and apply some of their attributes to the way we conduct ourselves, but even then, it must fit who we are in a genuine way. We can always find ways to improve who we are, but it must be real because we cannot fool ourselves and we surely cannot fool the people around us, especially as a Quarterback.

Eyes are on the Quarterback 24/7. People watch everything from the way he walks into the facilities, works out, drinks his sports beverage, puts on his jersey, his conduct in public, and of course his play and conduct on the field. The Quarterback's position is viewed as a position of leadership, and unless he is his authentic self, he will not be able to lead effectively because those he attempts to lead will see him as phony and will not take him seriously in any capacity. It is important that while seeking to discover his authentic self that he do so with an open and honest mind. A Quarterback should ask himself the question, "Who am I?" and then ask himself, "Who do I want to be?" As he thinks about who he is now, it is important that he is humble enough to write down his positive qualities and also those qualities he would like to improve as a person in everyday life and as a Quarterback. No one is perfect, but the best of leaders recognize or find ways to improve areas that need work and enhance the strengths they already have. A Quarterback cannot take the field and be a "rah-rah" type Quarterback if that is not in his nature, trying to emulate his favorite Quarterback on TV. He cannot take the field calm, cool, collected, and under control at the beginning of a game like his favorite Quarterback if he is out of control emotionally on the practice field. Everything he does from start to finish needs to be genuine.

Again, a Quarterback can improve or adopt certain qualities, but they must be authentic to who he is. If there is a quality that he wants to adopt because he thinks it will be beneficial, but it's not exactly who he is, he should take pride in adopting it and make it his own. There is no question that all competitors flip a switch from the time they are off the field to the time they arrive on the field, but it's important that both the on and off switches are authentic and recognizable.

Quarterback Exercise: Write down five personality traits that you like about yourself.

Like
1.
2.
3.
4.
5.

Quarterback Exercise: Write down five traits you have as a Quarterback on the field that you like and five traits you would want to change or adopt. Perhaps you have a favorite Quarterback who has traits that you can adopt and making it your own within your authentic self.

Like	Change/Adopt
1.	
2.	
3.	
4.	
5.	

Quarterback Exercise: Write down what you feel are your top five life values and also what you feel are the top five values a Quarterback should have.

Life	Quarterback
1.	
2.	
3.	
4.	
5.	

CHAPTER 7
The Ps of Preparation

Pride

> *"You're not some flash in the pan corner or receiver... or even Julian Washington. You're a goddamn quarterback! You know what that means? It's the top spot, kid. It's the guy who takes the fall. It's the guy everybody's looking at first–the leader of a team–who will support you when they understand you. Who will break their ribs and their noses and their necks for you, because they believe. 'Cause you make 'em believe. That's a quarterback."*
>
> —Any Given Sunday

This statement speaks volumes to what it means to take pride in playing the Quarterback position. This is not to say other positions on the field are not important, but it's just a fact that the Quarterback is the single-most important job on the field, and it should be a position that players take a great deal of pride in playing and improving daily in all aspects. The Quarterback should take one minute for himself and say the words, "I am a Quarterback." How does it feel to him? It does not matter if he is the starter or the backup; he needs to be proud of his title. Pride is not a bad thing if applied correctly. Pride is something that should fuel a player for the better every day. When he is proud to be a Quarterback of the team, he will prepare with a great deal of pride and relentlessness. He takes pride in being the guy everyone can look at and feel, "We got this, because we got him!" He takes pride in setting the example or tone for every meeting and practice session. He takes pride walking into the room first, taking the most notes, and working the hardest because more than anything, he has pride in being the best teammate possible for the team. When he takes pride in every aspect of his work, everyone else will follow.

The Quarterback should want others to take pride in having him as their Quarterback. There is not a better feeling than to hear a teammate say with pride, "He's our Quarterback." Even if he is a backup currently striving to become the starter, the pride he is taking into preparation, leadership, and so forth will speak volumes, and when he is on the field, they take as much pride in him as they do the current starting Quarterback. Pride is contagious, and when a Quarterback displays it in his preparation, it will show up in his play and everyone else's. Just as he wants his parents or family members to be proud of the person he becomes and proud of what he accomplishes off the field, he should strive for the same goals, feelings, and aspirations with his teammates, coaches, the program, and community he represents. If he takes pride in being the best person he can be off the field and in his preparation as a Quarterback, he will find others taking pride in going the extra mile for him.

M-QB Solution

- Take pride in being a Quarterback. It's the greatest position in sports.
- Take pride in your preparation, and truly work to improve every day.
- Take pride in being the best teammate you can possibly be.
- Pride is contagious

Patience

"A man who masters patience is master of everything else."

—George Savile

Mindful Quarterbacking is a practice, and like any practice, patience is required. By applying the M-QB principles, reminders, and exercises, the Quarterback will see the results of his practice unfold, and he will be able to live in the present moment and Quarterback one snap at a time. The best reminder for a Quarterback is that he will not be perfect in his practice, but he should also remember that as long as he is practicing, he is getting closer to being where he wants to be. There will be setbacks, but part of practicing Mindful Quarterbacking is utilizing the M-QB principles, reminders, and exercises to handle setbacks the best way he can. If he is using tools to handle the setbacks he faces, that itself is progress. Being patient in his development will also assist with his patience on the field with himself, coaches, and teammates and in everyday life.

Passion

"Passion is oxygen of the soul."

—Bill Butler

A player must have passion about his preparation as a Quarterback. If he lacks in his passion, he will lack in his progress. Passion does not mean he has to enjoy every second of preparation. Having passion means that he loves and cares about his position as a Quarterback enough to always do what is required to the best of his abilities, even when things are not going his way. Passion is about always finding one reason to hold on and keep moving forward when there are a hundred reasons to quit. Passion is remembering that he gets to play a game, prepare for a game, and be with teammates. Passion is finding every opportunity to celebrate successes and being motivated to improve on shortcomings. Passion is contagious and can set the tone of every meeting, film session, and practice long before he steps onto the field for game day. When a Quarterback has passion, he does everything he can to stay connected with what he loves, no matter how difficult things become. If he has enough passion in his preparation, progress will happen.

Perseverance

> *"If you can't fly then run, if you can't run then walk, if you can't walk then crawl, but whatever you do you have to keep moving forward."*
>
> —Martin Luther King, Jr.

Perseverance is arguably the most important aspect of preparation. There are going to be setbacks and struggles throughout the journey. Maybe he is the backup Quarterback trying to overtake the starting Quarterback. Maybe he is currently the starting Quarterback and is not exactly performing the way he would like. In either one of those situations, there are going to be times where he struggles and will have to always find it within himself to continue to push forward and overcome the challenge in front of him.

The greatest thing a Quarterback can do while facing a challenge is to learn from it, work in the present moment, envision success, understanding what he can control, being his authentic self, and most importantly, remembering that perfection is not expected and improvement can always happen as long as he works in the present moment and ignores the noise. Perseverance is a choice.

CHAPTER 8
The Cs of Competition

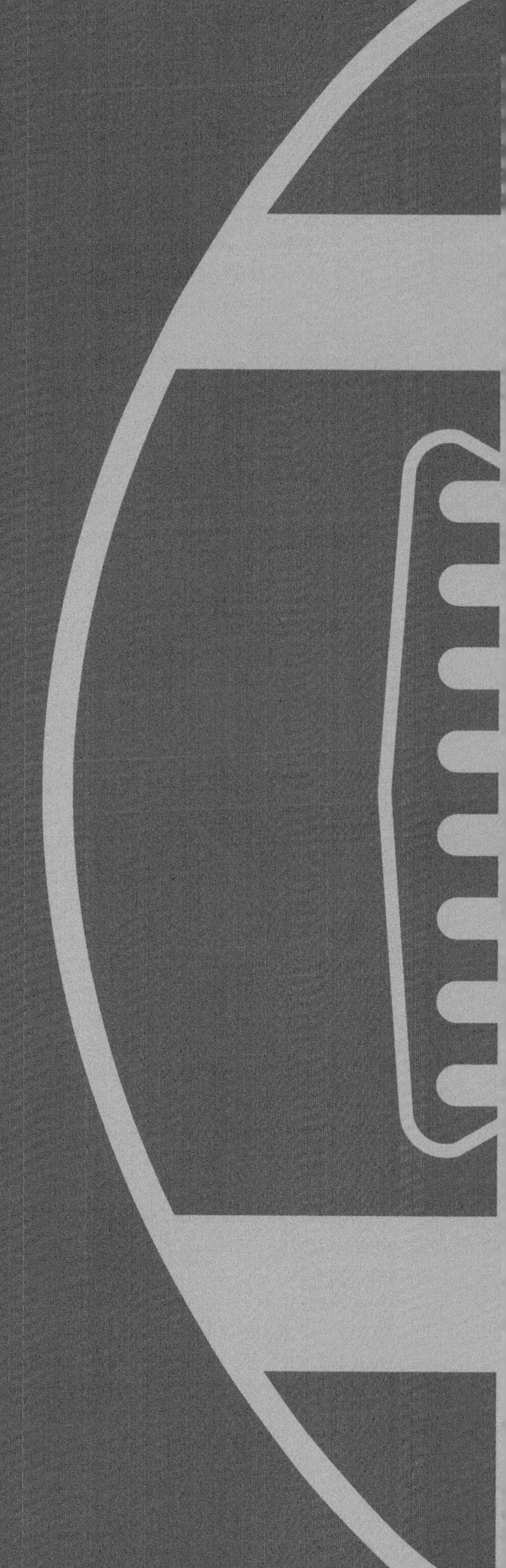

Coachable

"I feel sorry for people who know everything because they will never have that joyful feeling or experience of learning something new."

—Mindful Quarterbacking

Quarterbacks have to be coachable at all times. Being coachable starts with letting the ego-self go and tapping into the beginner's mind. I have seen countless Quarterbacks at all levels not make it as far as they could have simply because they were not coachable. They are players and their job is to play. Whether the Quarterback likes it or not, he is not the coach. The coach is the coach, and his job is to coach the players. The Quarterback's role as a player is to be coached, so he can play at his best for the betterment of the team. No matter how good of a player a Quarterback is or how much knowledge about the game he might have, he are not a coach, and it's highly likely (if not guaranteed) that he does not have more knowledge about the game of football than the coach. If he remains coachable, the coach is more likely to also gain respect for his knowledge of the game and at times even ask his thoughts and opinions on what he feels is best at particular times. Many coaches love to communicate football with coachable players who also have solid knowledge of the game because it helps everyone's chances of being successful.

The first step to being coachable is showing appreciation to the coach by understanding that they are more than likely trying to do their best for the Quarterback to help him reach his potential. The next step is to humble himself and realize that he does not, in fact, know it all. Even the best coaches of all-time have sincerely said that they do not know it all. So if the coach does not know it all, and knowledge of the game is their job, why would the Quarterback think he knows it all? The Quarterback must let the ego-self go and open his beginner's mind in order to gain knowledge, even if he already knows it. He must also understand that he is not ever going to be perfect at all times. When he accepts the fact the perfection is not attainable 24/7, it will help him be more open to coaching because the stresses and fantasies of perfection will not cloud his judgment and ability to listen.

Being aware of body language is also critical to begin coachable. This book has already covered briefly the impact body language can have on performance and how it impacts the way people view the Quarterback as a person and player; it is no different when it comes to being coachable. No coach enjoys coaching someone who is rolling their eyes, gritting their teeth, making angry faces, giving sarcastic looks, looking away while being spoken to, or chuckling disrespectfully. A player might be the greatest Quarterback anyone has seen in years, but if he cannot show the ability to take instruction and do exactly what he is told, if he thinks he is better than his coaches, his abilities might not ever be seen because the reality is that he is not in charge of playing time (the coach is), and no good coach is going to put up with a player (especially a Quarterback) who refuses to be coached and also displays non-coachable body language. When a player is coachable, coaches trust him and they can better work together. When a player is coachable, his knowledge of the game will become more respected, but he will also learn more about the game. When a player is not coachable, he cannot be trusted, and if he cannot be trusted, he is hurting his chances of playing and being successful. A coach's job is to coach, and a player's job is play, and they win as one.

M-QB Solution

- You are a Quarterback; your job is to play and listen. Your coach's job is to coach.
- Humble yourself. You do not know it all.
- Let go of the ego-self.
- Keep in mind that non-coachable players can't be trusted. Players who can't be trusted don't play.
- Remain coachable, and your coach will gain respect for your knowledge.
- Understand that your coach is doing their best for you and wants to succeed.

Communication

"As the leader, part of the job is to be visible and willing to communicate with everyone."

—Bill Walsh

The ability to communicate effectively is a must for any Quarterback. The ability to communicate with teammates and coaches at any given time is an important component to begin successful as a team. Communication does not mean simply talking or saying words. Communication is about thoroughly identifying the situation, finding the problem, and developing a solution as a team. Football is an emotional game, and no one feels pressure throughout a game more than a Quarterback because the ball is in his hands more than anyone on the field. Throughout a game, emotions can start to get the better of the Quarterback when things are not going his way. Heart rate skyrockets, breathing becomes rapid or out of control, and the ability to communicate effectively suffers because he is a prisoner of the moment and he begins communicating through frustration and anger rather than with reason and understanding. It's very important that the Quarterback observe his emotions before communicating, when anger or frustration is present in the mind.

Imagine that the Quarterback has had four chances to throw a touchdown pass and the receivers have flat out dropped them in the end zone, things just are not going the team's way, and frustration with them sets in because the Quarterback begins to imagine what could have been, the lead the team could have, and maybe even the ego-self kicks in and starts telling him that he could have great stats if they would just hold on to the ball. It is important that the Quarterback just not communicate, but that he communicates with consistency.

Communicating with consistency means that, in all situations, the Quarterback needs to have a routine or positive pattern of behavior that he, his coaches, and teammates can identify on how he will handle things when frustrated. If he becomes angry with a situation, it does not help to run and scream at teammates or coaches. They will stop listening to him, lose respect for him, stop playing for him, and if they are a coach, they are more likely to pull him out of the game. If his teammates will not play for him or respect him and the coaches do not play him, what good can he do for the team? Not only that, but everyone in the stands—young kids, television, recruiters, and newspaper reporters—sees his behavior and it's going to impact their perception of who he is as a player and most importantly as a person. An example of a routine would be the Quarterback going over to the sideline, using a couple Pre-Practice Meditations (Appendix B-2), and allowing the emotions of anger and frustration to slowly pass while observing things for what they are, regaining control of his emotions.

When the Quarterback feels he has regained control, he should walk over to his receivers and offer words of encouragement, show some compassion and understanding that they are not intentionally dropping balls, it's not personal toward them like his emotions make it out to be; they probably feel terrible about it and want to do well for him and the team. He should let them know that even though he is frustrated with their drops, he believes in them because they have done great things before or they are close. Also, he should always remind himself that he makes frustrating mistakes also. It is also important that the Quarterback and the coaches build a line of communication and an understanding of how they both communicate during competition, so that nothing is taken personally or out of context.

When the coach learns how the Quarterback best communicates and what helps him and what hurts him, he will more than likely adapt his communication with the Quarterback so that they can both handle solutions together, even in the toughest of times.

Quarterback Exercise: Write down five situations or events during a game that tend frustrate you.

1.
2.
3.
4.
5.
6.

Quarterback Exercise: Write down five sentences about what you think you can do to improve your communication with your teammates.

1.
2.
3.
4.
5.
6.

Quarterback Exercise: Write down five sentences about what you think you can do to improve your communication with your coaches.

1.
2.
3.
4.
5.
6.

M-QB Solution

- Remember that football is an emotional game.
- Before communicating, observe and calm your emotions.
- Use a sideline routine to regain control of your emotions.
- Keep in mind that yelling or screaming doesn't help anyone. It only hurts the situation.
- Offer words of encouragement when things go wrong.
- Be consistent in your communication. The more consistent you are, the more people will listen.

Confidence

"Confidence is the cornerstone of great performance and it comes from just one place: what we say to ourselves."

—Michael Gervais

For a Quarterback, having confidence in his preparation and abilities is the key to his success. The more confidence he has, the better chances he has of succeeding. The greatest way to gain confidence is by being prepared for the task at hand. The better a player performs, the more confidence he gains. However, sometimes a player begins to lose confidence in his abilities when things are not going as planned. One of the attributes of a Mindful Quarterback is that, even when things are not going as planned, he will remain confident that he will get things back on track and will improve with each opportunity he is given. Slumps happen, but maintaining a confident state of mind and displaying confident body language will take the Quarterback a long way. When things are not going as planned, oftentimes he might become prisoner of the moment in his emotions. For instance, if he has thrown five straight incomplete passes to open receivers and everyone, including himself, gets frustrated with him, oftentimes, the Quarterback can begin to lose his composure and confidence in himself and start to wonder if something is wrong with him, and his mind begins to think of what negative events are about to unfold.

When a Quarterback practices and displays confidence, a situation as just discussed will enable him to remind himself that he has performed well before, has overcome difficulty before, and can do so again. If he did not have the abilities to be a Quarterback, he would not be on the field. Quarterbacks at every level have struggles and, at times, lose some confidence in their abilities. What the best of the best do is regain their confidence before they take the field again. It's best for a Quarterback to remember something positive about his abilities when things aren't going well, rather than to reflect on how poorly things are going. Even if he throws several bad passes, he might want to say to himself, "I'll be alright. I've completed 10 in a row before, and I can do it again. Just follow the plan and play one snap at a time." Playing one snap at a time is critical to confidence.

When the Quarterback lives in the moment of each snap, disappointments are short-lived and success is recognized and experienced in its entirety. A Quarterback surrounding himself with positive and optimistic thinkers is another great way to remain confident. If the people around him, including teammates, are negative, he should either remove himself from that type of talk or be the one who invokes confidence in others. The Quarterback can give them the vision of having a great comeback with his words and body language and let them know he has confidence in their abilities and that temporary setbacks are not final results, just opportunities to make something special happen.

M-QB Solution

- Gain confidence by being prepared.
- Play one snap at a time. It's critical to regaining and maintaining confidence.
- Remain confident that you will get things back on track and will improve.
- Remind yourself that you have performed well before and can do so again.
- Talk positive to yourself. Choosing positive thinking is a choice. Practice it.

Calmness

"When a Quarterback remains calm, it makes the defense think a storm could still be coming their way."

—Mindful Quarterbacking

"Remain calm." It's a demand every Quarterback, despite how old they are or what level they play, has been given many times. A Quarterback has to remain calm. The key word is remain. There are times through practice and game time where everything is going to be going smoothly where there is no need for panic and simply nothing to take him out of his groove. As he will find out (if he hasn't already), remaining calm becomes a lot more difficult when things are going downhill or when the Quarterback are under duress, getting knocked down and hit. Most often, the environment around is not calm, and body language and thinking speeds up with the environment around him. Oftentimes, he may have a coach that is breathing down his neck, in his face, or screaming at him trying to figure out why he can't simply complete a five-yard hitch and he doesn't want to hear any excuses. The Quarterback looks up into the stands or begins wondering if people are talking about him. He may begin yelling at his teammates, trying to take some of the blame off his shoulders. The scenarios can go on forever.

The best way to remain calm is to slow down thinking. The Quarterback also needs to take into account the way others are feeling at particular times and to remember that everyone wants to win and other people are still developing when it comes to being calm during chaos. Most importantly, he knows how to remain calm; he just needs to remember and when he does, it's going to trickle down to his teammates, and it also impacts coaches in a positive way. The Quarterback should identify the situation for what it is, get the play, and just do what he's been coached to do. The best way to remain calm is to remember: "I can only control what I do." If he is giving his absolute best efforts, then that's all that matters. He should just remain calm and communicate with his teammates and coaches and compete is a calm, cool, and collected manner.

M-QB Solution

- Slow down your thinking.
- Observe your breathing and regulate it.
- Remaining calm helps others remain calm.

Consistency

"Leadership comes with consistency."

—Junior Seau

Everyone wants to be consistent in their performance. Consistency in behavior is a very overlooked trait. As a Quarterback, consistency is vital in every area, both on and off the field. Consistent behaviors will lead to having consistent performances. When players are consistently utilizing proper preparation, the more likely they are to succeed. When a Quarterback is consistent with positive leadership behaviors such as body language, communication, competiveness, and so forth, the more likely he is to succeed as a leader and the more likely those around him will go the extra mile for him on and off the field. Consistency does not mean perfection. Mistakes and setbacks will happen. Quarterbacks who are consistent are able to remind themselves of what they must do to stay consistent and also recover consistently when things are not going as planned and by utilizing the tools and resources they practice regularly. When he practices regularly, with purpose and passion, he will find performances becoming more consistent and at times excelling beyond what he thought possible.

Consistency and availability are very important aspects of Quarterbacking. Consistency can fall into the good or bad. If a Quarterback is consistently good, it is an indication of his work ethic. If he is consistently bad or inconsistent and simply has a few "flash in the pan" performances, it is an indication of his work ethic.

In terms of communication, if a Quarterback rages at his teammates for making mistakes one day and are kind to them another, it is an indication of inconsistent leadership. If he shows passion on the field one week and then is lethargic the next, it is an indication of inconsistent leadership also.

A Quarterback should be consistent in every area of his life and always looking to improve on his consistencies. It all starts at home, in the community, in the classroom, followed by off-season and in-season workouts, film session, and practices. Every Quarterback can have a few "big time" games in their career, but his coach would likely much rather he have a season of consistent modest stats and productive games rather than a few "big time" games and inconsistency throughout the rest of the season. Consistency is all areas can help give the team the greatest chance of being successful.

Consistency vs. Inconsistency by the Numbers

Quarterback 1	Completions	Attempts	Yards	Touchdowns	Interceptions	Result
Game 1	11	15	110	2	0	W
Game 2	14	17	180	0	0	W
Game 3	20	25	150	2	1	W
Game 4	28	35	200	3	1	W
Game 5	18	23	195	1	0	W

Quarterback 2	Completions	Attempts	Yards	Touchdowns	Interceptions	Result
Game 1	25	40	290	3	3	L
Game 2	32	37	500	6	1	W
Game 3	10	35	80	0	2	L
Game 4	15	34	155	1	1	L
Game 5	20	45	350	2	3	L

Quarterback 1 Through Five Games:

- Does not have gaudy statistics, but Quarterback 1 is highly consistent in productivity.
- Has a touchdown:interception ratio of 8:2.
- Has thrown for 835 yards.

Quarterback 2 Through Five Games:

- Has put up big stats in terms on yards and touchdowns, but is very inconsistent in productivity.
- Quarterback 2 has a touchdown:interception ratio of 12:10.
- Has thrown for 1,375 yards.

Statistics or big stats do not always determine the outcome of the game. However, it is safe to assume that Quarterback 1 provided his team with a better chance of winning than Quarterback 2 did because of his consistency. Winning is the only statistic that matters. Most importantly, Quarterback 1 has more than likely has displayed a better work ethic to become so consistent and productive. As a Quarterback, training to be consistent in eliminating turnovers is critical. The ball is always in his hands, and the less he gives it away and the more consistently he plays, the better chance he and the team have of being successful. There is nothing wrong with having "big time" games and putting up gaudy stats, it is fun and boosts confidence, but it is best to do so with productivity. A Quarterback should strive to be the most consistently productive player possible in his leadership and play of the field.

M-QB Solution

- Practice consistent behavior on and off the field.
- Always work on consistency and always be available to your team any time you can.
- It's all about consistent productivity, not gaudy stats.
- Remember that consistency and availability are two very important aspects of Quarterbacking.

Control

"It is a very important part of life that we must always keep things in perspective so that we can maintain emotional control."

—John Wooden

This principle (control) is about the Quarterback controlling himself and his emotions and learning to stay in control of himself with the things or circumstances he cannot control. Players have been told at one point or another in their life to control themselves or to take control of the situation. Oftentimes, we mistake taking control of the situation as needing to forge our will in every facet of the game. A Mindful Quarterback sees taking control as returning his mind to everything he can control within himself mentally and in his physical performance. Being in control also involves not getting too hyped that he wastes energy or begins to lose focus because of the whirlwind of emotions. Remaining in control does not mean he will not have emotions; it simply means always seeking to find the center or balance within himself no matter how good or tough the situation might be. A great way to always check inner balance is to evaluate what he can and cannot control, and doing so will eliminate half the problem of his emotions.

Let's say the team is in a shootout, and neither defense can stop the other from scoring. The Quarterback might have thrown a big touchdown pass or used his feet to score late in this high-scoring affair. Everyone, including the Quarterback, is full of emotion and celebrating. Celebrating is great, but he has to now bring himself back to balance with his thoughts and emotions because the game is not yet over, the team might need his energy again if the defense cannot stop the opponents their next drive. Flipping the script, imagine the team are in the same shootout, except the Quarterback are on the sideline watching the opposing Quarterback lead his team down for a later score. It is upsetting to watch them celebrate, but he cannot lose control and waste mental or physical energy by raging, yelling, getting angry, and so forth. It's time for him to bring his emotions back to balance and lead his team down for a score.

The Quarterback has no control over how the opposing team plays. He does have control over how he plays, and balancing the emotions of the game within himself—no matter which side of the coin he is on—is key to the team's success. When a Quarterback learns to truly find balance within himself and can identify what is in and out of his control, he will find playing the Quarterback position to not only be smoother mentally, but also much more enjoyable. If he can gain control of himself first, he will have better control of his performance, and the more control he has of his performance, the better chance the team has of being successful.

M-QB Solution

- Remind yourself of what you can control.
- Don't waste mental energy getting too upset.
- Don't waste physical energy getting too hyped.
- Balance your emotions.

Competitive

"Don't get angry; get competitive!"

—Mindful Quarterbacking

Being competitive is not something that starts once players reach the football field on game day. Everything a Quarterback does off the field in everyday life and in practice contributes to how competitive he is. Being competitive is a lifestyle. The greatest competitors are always competing with themselves to improve their abilities before competing with others. Great competitors impose their will to accomplish any challenge placed in front of them and utilize mental endurance to succeed. Competing at all times also allows them to not focus on the past. Great competitors are so focused on improving and coming back to be victorious and know that taking their minds back to what just happened will only hinder their abilities to remain in a competitive frame of mind. The Quarterback is learning about Mindful Quarterbacking, and mindfulness is all about the present moment and what he can accomplish in each moment that is present. Although being in the here and now is the main objective, it does not mean he cannot allow certain events to fuel his competitive drive. If he throws an interception that gets returned for a touchdown, it is natural for anger or frustrations to set in and for it to be on his mind for a moment. However, when things such as that happen on the field, the best course is get competitive, not angry.

Too often, people associate anger with being competitive, and they are not the same thing. When referring to an athlete who just experienced a setback or something they did not like and they follow it up with a great response with their play, you will often hear a commentator on television say, "Look out, he's getting angry." What the commentators should be saying is, "Look out, he's getting more competitive." When someone performs out of anger, they lose control of their purpose and lose themselves in their emotions and what is happening around them. We have all seen what happens when someone responds with anger, and it often results in poor play, terrible sportsmanship, penalties, fights, heated arguments, and even ejections from the game. We have all also seen what happens when someone responds with being more competitive and how well they keep their emotions in check, body language under control, still playing the game the right way, using clear communication and keeping their competitive nature or taking it to another level.

Every snap a Quarterback takes needs to be done with calmness, composure, and a competitive approach on the practice field and during game time. When things are not going his way and he becomes angry, he should utilize Mindful Quarterbacking meditations to regroup his thoughts and remain competitive. Again, there is nothing wrong with being fueled by setbacks as long as they are utilized to remain competitive in the present moment. When a Quarterback remains competitive and focused on the current snap, the past setbacks will naturally begin to fade.

Remember, each snap is a new beginning, so the Quarterback should maximize it with competitiveness while being his authentic self. The more competitive he is, the better chance he has of improving and the better chance the team has of being successful.

M-QB Solution

- Don't get angry; get competitive.
- Remain competitive. It will help you stay in the present moment.
- Don't allow anger to control your emotions and cause you to lose focus on the team's purpose.
- No matter what happens, always play the game the right way.
- Keep in mind that using anger can result in you playing poorly and also being ejected.
- Take every snap and always display calmness, composure, and competiveness.

Compassion

"Compassion is passion with heart."

—Tom Krause

Displaying compassion towards self and teammates is often the most overlooked aspect of competition. This does not mean players should not remain competitive, but compassion can often be a useful tool during competition, especially during times where the competition is really heating up. When something does not go our way during the heat of battle (such as a dropped pass on a key down, a fumble, interception etc.), we often allow the anger we have toward the events that are happening around us to also come out on those around us. During a heated battle, everyone is on edge because the inevitable result is that there can only be one winner, and in football, you only get to play once a week, which only makes the emotions and the stakes higher. The greatest of competitors also find a way to display a level of compassion during the heat of battle both with themselves and their teammates. Many of the Quarterback's teammates are going to look at him for a level of compassion or understanding while remaining competitive. Simply letting his teammates know that he believes in their abilities is a way of showing compassion. If a running back fumbles at the most critical time, the Quarterback like many others will be disappointed with the outcome of the play, but as soon as he allows the frustrations to pass and bring his mind to the next series or snap, he should quickly go over to his teammate and give him words of encouragement, let him know that everyone (including himself) has made mistakes, that mistakes do not define him, and that the Quarterback knows who he is and what he's capable of doing.

A Quarterback having compassion toward himself on the field comes down to understanding that he not perfect and taking the time to refocus himself at any given time. Having compassion toward himself is removing the negative self-talk from his mind and not beating himself up over the past, no matter how fresh it is. Having compassion toward himself is remembering who he is as a person and as a Quarterback and remembering that all the positives he has done can be done again. When a person has compassion toward themselves, they understand that unfortunate circumstances are not a result of who they are as a person; they are a result of many things, some of which they cannot control. Of course, when things do not go our way, we get upset, but there is no evidence that shows when a player stays angry about the previous play that it enhances their game. I believe the opposite to be true, and that is when a player simply identifies the mistakes he made and does not hold on to the past emotionally and brings his mind to the present, his game enhances. Displaying compassion is something that can be practiced along with working on selfless acts off the field, and it will carry over in competition. The most compassionate of people feel for others who are struggling, and they feel overcome with joy when they see others succeed and genuinely want the best results to come out of everyone with whom they surround themselves.

For a Quarterback, applying compassion to his leadership arsenal is going to help him grow in big ways on and off the field, especially in the heat of battle. Compassion is not weak; compassion takes strength and courage.

M-QB Solution

- Display compassion. It shows strength.
- When things go bad, offer words of encouragement to your teammates.
- Have compassion towards yourself by removing negative self-talk.
- Remember that no one is perfect.
- Appreciate the efforts everyone is giving toward a common goal.

Courage

> *"You learn you can do your best even when it's hard, even when you're tired and maybe hurting a little bit. It feels good to show some courage."*
>
> —Joe Namath

Courage can be defined in many different ways. Courage is doing something we don't necessarily want to do or doing something that can put us in harm's way for the betterment of others and for a greater cause or outcome. Courage is about facing fears or uncomfortable situations head on. A good example of courage for a Quarterback is getting up after being hit time and time again or standing in the pocket and delivering a strike to the wide receiver, knowing that he is about to take a hit from a free running linebacker coming right up the middle, without flinching, and having more focus on the team's success than the pain he might experience from a solid hit. The old saying "Pain is temporary, but pride and victory are forever" is a great statement that defines courage. Courage is also about not being afraid of who we are and not giving into the pressures or thoughts surrounding the circumstances. A Quarterback who has the belief that the team can come back and win the game should have the courage to say so ("Hey, I know we can come back and win this! Get on my back and let's see what happens. We got this!"). I have had experiences where a Quarterback will tell me after a game that he really believed we would come back and win a game, and when I ask him if he told the rest of the team, he says he didn't, and when I ask him why, the reply is usually: "I don't know, I guess I was too worried they would think I was crazy" or "I'm not sure they believe in me." A player might have the fire in his soul to want to make a great comeback, and having the courage to share that belief is an important element of Quarterbacking, but it must be real and genuine, not artificial fantasies or emotions.

Courage has a unique way of inspiring others to perform at their best, and in some ways to create a subconscious courage in others and a subconscious belief that they can overcome whatever challenge is in front of them. I have seen time and time again where a Quarterback who stands in the pocket delivers pass after pass after pass as if nothing can stop him, all the while getting hit hard every snap. There is something within the makeup of us as humans or in the brain that makes us want to rally around people who show courage, and when teammates see it, they will eventually respond.

One of the most courageous plays in football history to me happened in Super Bowl XXXII when John Elway and the Denver Broncos played Bret Favre and the Green Bay Packers. The Green Bay Packers were defending world champions, and the Denver Broncos were seeking their first Super Bowl victory in franchise history. Quarterback John Elway had been to the Super Bowl on three different occasions and been on the losing end of all three, and it would be until Elway was 37 years old before the Broncos made it back, but the Green Bay Packers were heavily favored to defeat Denver. During Super Bowl XXXII, the Broncos faced a critical third-and-six deep in the red zone. The game was tied, but the Packers had all the momentum. Just before John Elway received the shotgun snap, he quickly identified he had nowhere to go with the football, and he began scrambling. Elway was no young or fleet-footed Quarterback, but as he took off, he realized that four Green Bay Packers defenders were in front of him and going to stop him a couple yards short. Elway, like most Quarterbacks, usually slides in the situation and settles for the field goal. Everyone–the Broncos' players and coaches, the Packers' players and coaches, and everyone watching around the world, including myself–thought Elway was about to slide because he had four Packers defenders closing in on him. Rather than slide, Elway leaped into the air trying to pick up the first down, was hit by three of the four defenders in front of him and was literally spun in the air like a helicopter. It was a play that everyone describes as almost happening in slow motion. When Elway got up off the turf and realized he reached the first down marker, he got up a pumped his first to the sideline as the entire stadium erupted. His teammates all ran over to him with enthusiasm high-fiving him, hugging him, and tapping him on the helmet. It didn't just inspire his teammates; it inspired people in the stands and watching at home. It was the ultimate "wow" moment. If you were not cheering for a team in the Super Bowl before that play, you were pulling for the Broncos then.

That courageous play, as many of the Broncos players said, made them all believe that there was no way they could lose that game despite being the underdogs, and it elevated everyone's game because John Elway did not have to do that, most Quarterbacks never had at that point in time on a stage of that magnitude. Elway was already a millionaire and already considered one of the greatest to play the game and he was much older than many of the guys on the field, but he displayed the courage his team needed, and that play helped propel the Broncos to a 31-24 Super Bowl victory. I am sure the play didn't feel good, but the joy of winning his first Super Bowl and inspiring his team trumped any pain or fears. Courage is a choice.

Quarterback Exercise: Write down three times that you have displayed courage on the field. Why did you choose to show courage in that situation?

1.
2.
3.

Quarterback Exercise: Write down three times that you have displayed courage off the field. Why did you choose to show courage in that situation?

1.
2.
3.

his team [illegible] and [illegible] play [illegible] the [illegible] Super Bowl [illegible] the [illegible] first Super Bowl [illegible] Courage [illegible]

[illegible] times that you have displayed courage on the [illegible]?

Quarterback [illegible] times that you have displayed courage off the field? Why [illegible] courage in that situation?

CHAPTER 9
The Three Elements

Three Elements Structure

In recent years, the Mindful Quarterbacking principles have been restructured after Shauna Shapiro's model for mindfulness practitioners; she is a professor at Santa Clara University, a clinical psychologist, and an internationally recognized expert in mindfulness. Shapiro categorized mindfulness practice into three parts, which are also the three elements Mindful Quarterbacking (M-QB) has adopted. Those three elements are: intention, attention, and attitude. Within each of those elements, the M-QB principles will be placed.

Although Mindful Quarterbacking has always had its principles, adopting Shapiro's three elements of mindfulness over the last few years has greatly complemented the M-QB principles and gives the M-QB principles a greater sense of identity, goal setting structure, and overall structured purpose. It helps greatly that many of the M-QB principles are also many of the same principles of mindfulness.

Next, you will gain an understanding of how the three elements have helped structure mindfulness and the Mindful Quarterbacking principles and how the three elements (intention, attention, and attitude) bring them together.

Intention

Intention sets the tone. It gives the vision for what is possible and all we're striving to accomplish. Having the intention to accomplish a particular goal or task also provides confidence because they remind us why we're practicing. Intention does not mean that every goal will be obtained, but it provides direction or a map for the direction we wish to go. If we don't have an intention, we cannot start, and going somewhere unintentionally leaves us lost. Having an intention is the first step toward accomplishment. Intention reminds us of what is most important at that moment.

Quarterback Example

Let's say the Quarterback wants to have the intention to become a better leader for the team, and one of the ways he chooses to do that is by being less judgmental of his teammate's mistakes and not allowing his mistakes to get him so upset and take him out of the present moment. He must first tell himself, "Today, I want to focus on being a better leader for my teammates, and I want to do this by being non-judgmental." He has now set the tone for his goal and has set himself into the direction he wants to go. He also has confidence in obtaining his goal of becoming a better leader and being non-judgmental because he has direction.

Attention

Attention is your present moment awareness of what is going on around us internally and externally. When we pay attention or give something our full attention, we can better assess the situation around us and the emotion, feelings, or sensations within ourselves. We must give attention some attention itself by using tools that help us obtain present moment awareness and for us to properly and effectively meet our objective (intention). Attention does not simply mean seeing something; it means to view, evaluate, or do something with a calm and collected alertness. Without giving our full attention, we cannot truly obtain our intention fully.

Quarterback Example

Sticking with the example of wanting to become a better leader for the team, the Quarterback should think about what he should give his attention. For example, he can choose to have and display patience with his offensive linemen and himself when mistakes happen. He should work on giving patience his full attention. If he or another player makes a mistake or something goes wrong, he should understand that there is always time to improve, and spending that time upset does no one any good. A way to go about doing this would be to gather his linemen and say, "I know it can be frustrating for us all when mistakes happen, but let's focus on having patience with each other, and we will get the ball rolling eventually." He has now given patience a platform that requires his full attention.

Attitude

Attitude is the way we choose to approach our intentions and how we give attention. Our attitude in many ways should be consistent or compatible with what our intentions are. It's important to remember that we are in full control over the attitude we bring into each situation. Most of the time, we allow the experience or the situation to dictate our attitude rather than just observing the experience purely for what it is. To "have an attitude" isn't a bad thing; it's something that we simply need to pay attention to and make a conscious decision to bring the best attitude for the present situation.

Quarterback Example

As discussed, the Quarterback has decided to become a better leader and be less judgmental. He has also decided to utilize patience with himself and his teammates to assist him in being less judgmental. Now he must decide the attitude he wishes to bring. Let's say he chose trust. He will trust that his intention will work out for the best, and he will trust that by giving patience his full attention, things will turn out for the best. When showing trust, he and those around him begin to feed off of it, and trust turns into belief. This doesn't mean all will be perfect, but having a non-judgmental intention, giving patience his full attention, and displaying an attitude of trust can only increase the team's chances of success.

CHAPTER 10

M-QB Weekly Practice Goal Setting

Weekly Practice Goals

Earlier in this playbook, Chapter 2 covered controllable goals and examples about what a Quarterback can and cannot control. Weekly Practice Goals (WPGs) are fully within a Quarterback's control, and the M-QB principles and the three elements will help guide him in choosing, following, and executing the WPGs he sets for himself. As a reminder, the M-QB principles can all be categorized within the three elements and are also interchangeable.

Second, the blank boxes (Custom) in the M-QB principles table are for filling in a player's own principle or goal that he wishes to accomplish. An example of utilizing the M-QB principles and three elements will be presented in Table 10-1. Something else to keep in mind is that there is absolutely nothing wrong with repeating the same M-QB principles, having the same goals or created combinations. The Quarterback is encouraged to find his own creative approach and stick with what works, no different than the best pass or run play in a playbook, which is why a number of blank boxes are left for creativity.

Day of the Week	Intention	Attention	Attitude
Monday	Calmness	Breathing	Patience
Tuesday	Coachable	Trust	Beginner's Mind
Wednesday	Improve Ball Placement (Custom)	Confidence	Patience
Thursday	Improve Leadership (Custom)	Passion	Non-Judging

Table 10-1. Example of filling out daily practice goals using the M-QB principles

When you turn to the appendix, there will be several mindfulness meditations to utilize Monday through Thursday. Lastly, always remember any chapter that discusses an M-QB principle is available as a reminder to refresh a Quarterback's memory of their importance and to quickly reference when assistance in a particular area is needed.

Mindful Quarterbacking is a practice, and the more a player practices something, the better he will become. The M-QB principles table is spread out so that the Quarterback can take his time thoroughly looking and thinking through daily goals and what he would like to achieve, along with encouraging creativity. The WPGs are outlined for the high school Quarterback. A college Quarterback or coach can simply add an extra day to the routine. For a professional Quarterback or coach, feel free to add an extra day or two to the routine.

In my experience using the Mindful Quarterbacking approach, the vast majority of my Quarterbacks have customized goals or principles categorized under the intention and attitude elements. When a Quarterback is first starting out choosing an

M-QB principle and determining to which element to apply it, he can keep it simple if he'd like. He should not overthink it, and go with what comes natural. He will find interchangeable combinations that work for him with the M-QB principles only and within his own creativity. It is not mandatory to have an intention, attention, and attitude all working toward the same goal; sometimes he might simply want to focus on each of them as separate goals, and that is perfectly okay. I have had Quarterbacks go weeks where they create their own intention, attention, and attitude and have each of the three elements working together toward a daily goal as they are intended to be used. I have also had Quarterbacks create daily goals where their intention, attention, and attitude are working separately, and that is perfectly fine also because they still execute those things within the confines of the Mindful Quarterbacking lifestyle.

As previously mentioned, the appendix includes Monday through Thursday pre-practice mindfulness meditations. Other helpful resources include the Three Elements Daily Practice Goal Sheet (Table 10-2), where Quarterbacks can fill in their intention, attention, and attitude goals with an M-QB principle for each day; a Practice Reflection Sheet (Table 10-3), where Quarterbacks can record their thoughts about their days and their progress; and Daily Reflection Questions (Table 10-4), which provides Quarterbacks with specific questions to consider as they reflect. (Copies of these forms are also included in the appendix.) Quarterbacks are strongly encouraged to take the time to write their reflections and also write out their responses to the questions because it will provide them the opportunity to look back at their progress. However, if a Quarterback is ever in a situation where he is unable to write his responses, he can just take time when appropriate to sit and reflect on the questions and answer them to himself. In addition to these tools, M-QB guided imagery and other exercises are provided in Appendix A.

Three Elements Pre-Practice Goal Sheet		
Week ____	**Week ____**	**Week ____**
Monday	**Monday**	**Monday**
Intention	Intention	Intention
Attention	Attention	Attention
Attitude	Attitude	Attitude
Tuesday	**Tuesday**	**Tuesday**
Intention	Intention	Intention
Attention	Attention	Attention
Attitude	Attitude	Attitude
Wednesday	**Wednesday**	**Wednesday**
Intention	Intention	Intention
Attention	Attention	Attention
Attitude	Attitude	Attitude
Thursday	**Thursday**	**Thursday**
Intention	Intention	Intention
Attention	Attention	Attention
Attitude	Attitude	Attitude

Table 10-2. Three elements pre-practice goal sheet

Week ____: Practice Reflection Sheet
Monday
Tuesday
Wednesday
Thursday

Table 10-3. Practice reflection sheet

Practice Reflection Question Sheet
What principles did you apply today?
Why did you choose those principles?
Did any of the principles you chose come into use today? How?
What went well for you and/or the team today at practice?
Do you feel you were fully present during practice today?
What do you remember most from practice today?
What internal or external distractions came up during practice?
What did you do to handle any distractions or issues that arose?
Did you meet your intention(s) today?
Did you pay full attention to what you wanted?
Did you bring and maintain the attitude you wanted?
Did you give your absolute best efforts today?
What do you want to improve on?
What do you want to continue to do well?
(Final practice of the week question) Overall, do you feel you made improvements as a Quarterback this week? In what areas?

Table 10-4. Practice reflection question sheet

CHAPTER 11
Approaching Game Time

Game Time Goals

Game Time Goals (GTGs) is similar to the WPGs approach with a few differences in the approach to setting goals, charts, and questions. The Quarterback will want to keep things as similar as possible on game days to the way he approaches practice, only he will want to work on shifting his mind and attention to game time demands, challenges, and environment. The emphasis of his GTGs will be utilizing the Cs of Competition to evaluate himself.

Remember, the GTGs need to be about what he can control, not what he can't control. The diagrams that follow are to be filled out after the game. Outside of the Cs of Competition, the Quarterback should feel free to apply some of the other principles (custom) as goals or his own custom goals. He should always strive to apply the Cs of Competition and evaluate himself on them after the game.

It's important for the Quarterback to remember to choose the few goals that he wants to focus on (custom) and that he can always apply to M-QB principles throughout the game even if he did not write them down as a goal that week. With practicing the Mindful Quarterbacking approach, he will find that he begins to naturally apply most, if not all, of the M-QB principles without having to think twice about it.

Appendix B includes a daily game time approach guide to help the Quarterback manage his mindset throughout the day leading up to kickoff, after kickoff, and after the game ends. The M-QB Game Time Self-Evaluation Sheet in Table 11-1 will show an example of what the sheet looks like and how to fill it out, and Table 11-2 provides questions to answer any time after the game ends.

Game ______ : M-QB Game Time Self-Evaluation Sheet				
M-QB Principle	The Whole Time	Most of the Time	Some of the Time	Not at All
Coachable		X		
Communication	X			
Confidence		X		
Calmness			X	
Consistency		X		
Control			X	
Competitive	X			
Courage		X		
Compassion			X	
(Custom)				
(Custom)				
(Custom)				
(Custom)				

Table 11-1. M-QB Game Time Self-Evaluation Sheet

Game ______ : M-QB Game Time Reflection Questions
Did you meet your goals?
Did any of the Cs of Competition come into use today? How?
What M-QB or custom principles did you apply?
Why did you choose those principles?
What during the game went well for you and/or the team?
Do you feel you were fully present during the game?
What do you remember most from the game today?
What internal or external distractions came up during practice?
What did you do to handle any distractions or issues that arose?
Did you pay full attention to what you wanted?
Did you bring and maintain the attitude you wanted?
Did you give your absolute best efforts?
What principles do you want to apply next time?
What can you do to build on or improve your performance?
Overall thoughts and reflection from the game?

Table 11-2. M-QB Game Time Time Reflection Questions

CHAPTER 12
Distractions

This chapter provides a series of quarterback exercises to help quarterbacks think about how they can apply M-QB principles in various situations both on and off the field.

Off the Field

Situation 1

You come home from a long day at practice and are simply exhausted. You didn't have the greatest day of practice, and the school day didn't start off great either after you got back your test score and saw it was far below your expectations. You walk into the front door and within minutes are bombarded with questions about how your day went, how practice went, and you have family members seeking your attention and also wanting to have a piece of your time. Your mind is spinning out of control because your mind is filled up with everything that happened before you came home that day. You begin to feel frustration set in and just want people to back off and give you space. It's been a long day.

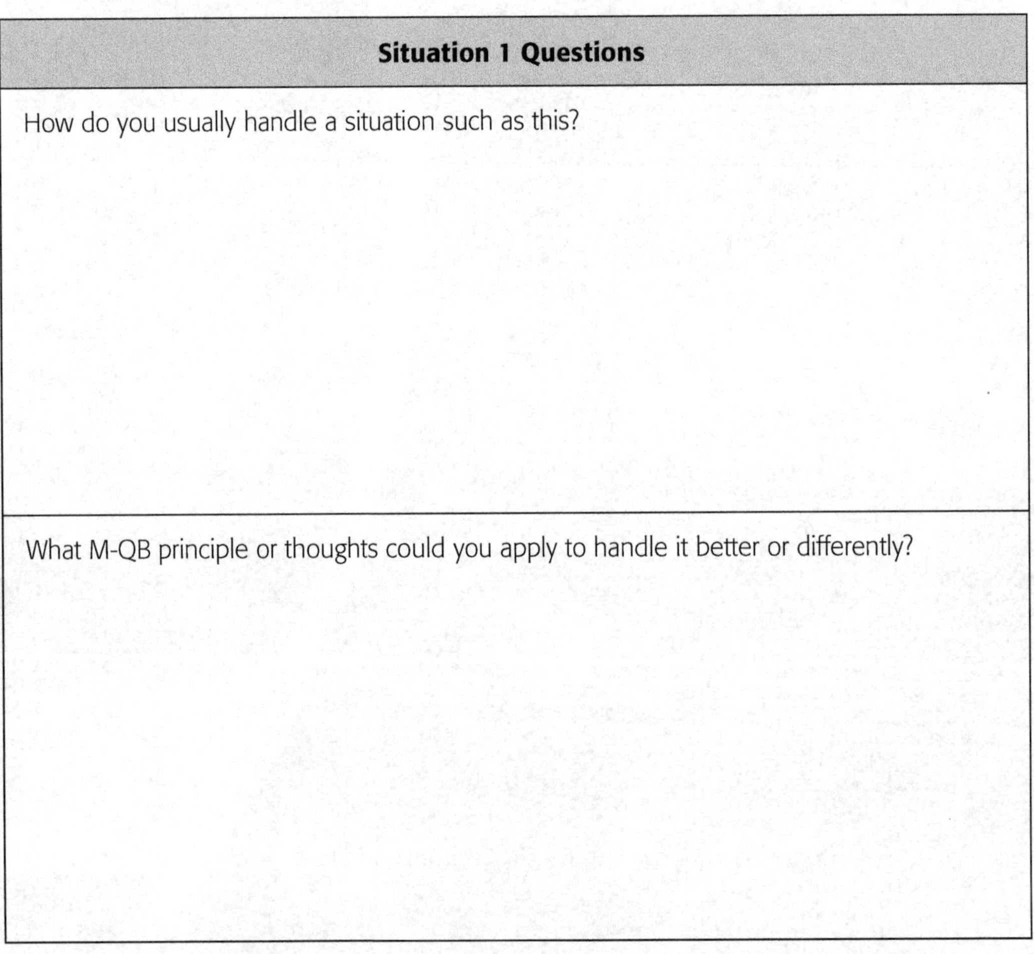

Situation 1 Questions
How do you usually handle a situation such as this?
What M-QB principle or thoughts could you apply to handle it better or differently?

Situation 2

It's Monday, and the day seems to be going relatively smoothly. You're in an upbeat mood, fully in the present moment, and have felt a sense of flow throughout the day. You walk into class just a few minutes early and are prepared to take class head on. When you sit down, a couple of people in your class begin to heckle you about the game last weekend and laugh at the fact you didn't play well. They begin to mock you being the Quarterback and do everything they can to remind you of all the bad plays that happened over the weekend and only talk about how much the football team has struggled to win this season. Your mind begins to flash back to all of the negatives that you're being reminded of from the last game and the anger you have toward the people heckling you. You begin to come out of the present moment and also your thoughts of anger have you imagining losing it on those who are heckling you.

Situation 2 Questions
How do you usually handle a situation such as this?
What M-QB principle or thoughts could you apply to handle it better or differently?

Situation 3

The local newspaper has chosen your program for a featured sports story. The newspaper makes you the spotlight player to conduct an interview and would like your thoughts and opinions on the upcoming game. The next day, the newspaper provides a lot of thoughts and opinions about how well you've played so far this season, but there are also several thoughts and opinions the newspaper gave on the struggles a few of your teammates are having this season. You are aware that everyone reads the newspaper and notice that the teammates who the newspaper mentioned are pretty upset that they were mentioned in a negative context. When you go back and closely read the article, you notice the newspaper is mostly praising you and bashing everyone else. The local news station wants to follow up on what the newspaper did and conduct a TV interview with you right before practice, which will be seen later that night.

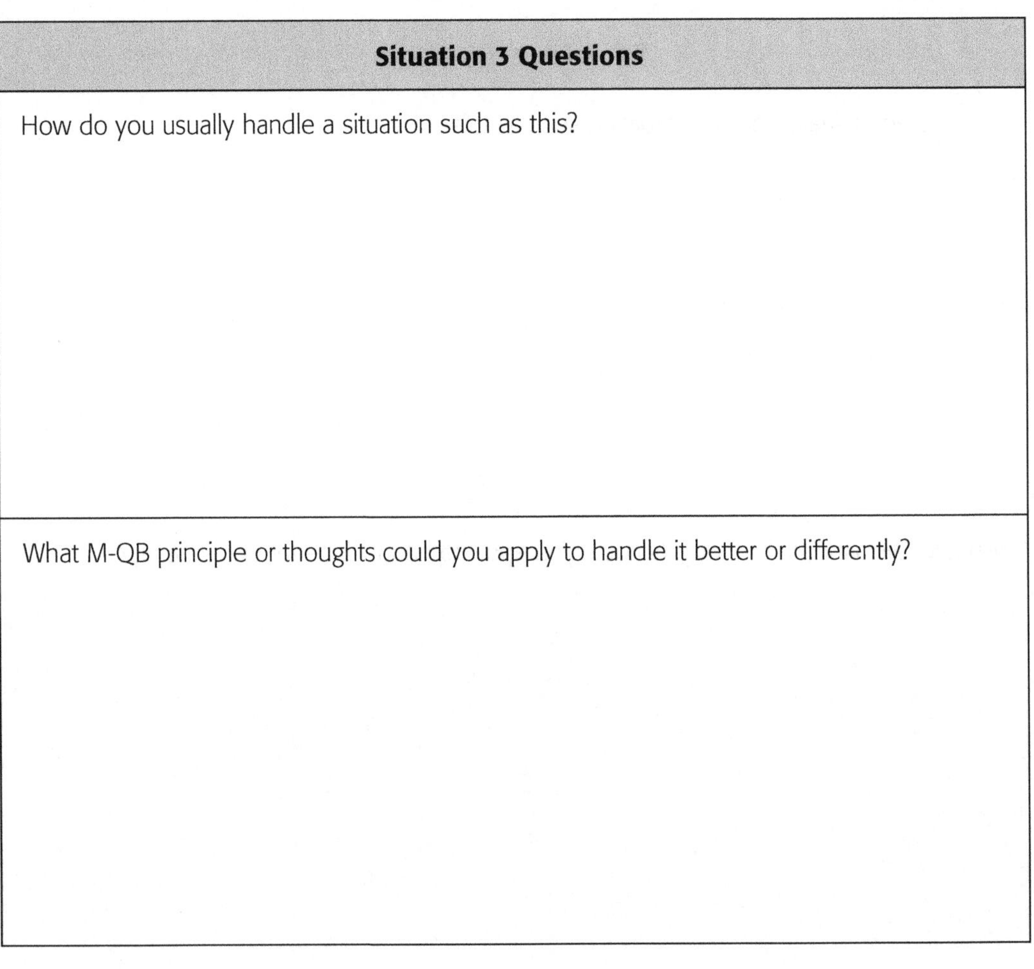

Situation 3 Questions
How do you usually handle a situation such as this?
What M-QB principle or thoughts could you apply to handle it better or differently?

Situation 4

It is the night before a game, and you're at home with your feet up, trying to relax and practicing your breathing exercises, preparing mentally and reviewing the game plan. You feel pretty good about where your mind is and are excited to play tomorrow. Later that night, you get several phone calls from friends and a couple of teammates who want you to go out with them to a party downtown, and they promise you won't be out too late. You are unsure if that is something you want to do, especially the night before a game. You are especially disappointed that some of your teammates are choosing to go out the night before a game and wish they would just stay home or relax until after the game is over. You do not want to exclude yourself from the team, but you also do not want to go out the night before a game, and you want to express your concerns to your teammates about them going out the night before a game, but you don't want to create animosity by expressing yourself.

Situation 4 Questions
How do you usually handle a situation such as this?
What M-QB principle or thoughts could you apply to handle it better or differently?

On the Field

Situation 1

You are out at practice working on the inside run period. Your coach gives you the play, and you go into the huddle and let everyone know that the snap count is on two and to make sure they stay onside until the ball is snapped. You break the huddle, jog to the line of scrimmage, and begin your cadence. On the first hut or go call, one of your offensive linemen false starts, and you have to reset the play. You remind the lineman that the snap is on two and to not false start. You again go into your cadence, and once again the same lineman false starts. Everyone groans, sighs, and begins shouting at him. He cannot believe it himself and has his hands on his head and begins to punch himself on the helmet with his fist out of frustration. You are also frustrated, as the coach asks everyone to huddle up again to start the play over; the team is not going anywhere until the play is run correctly.

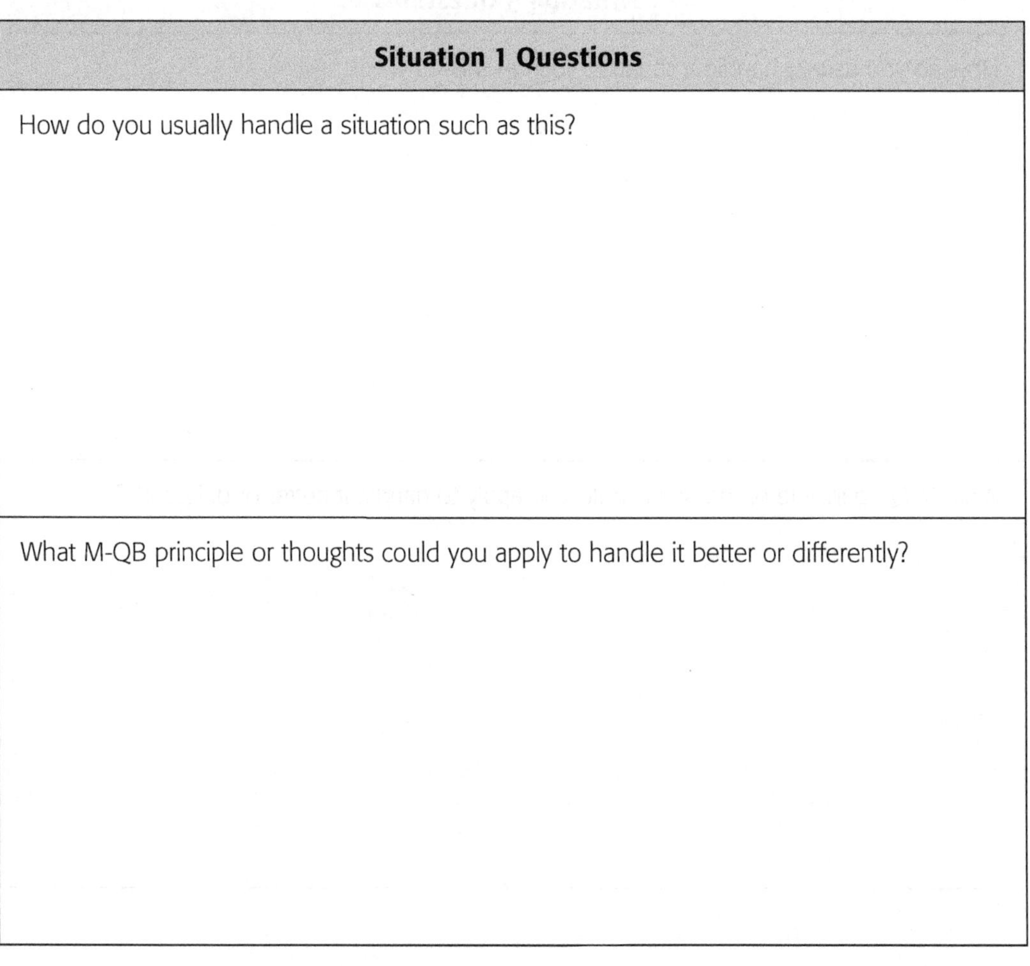

Situation 1 Questions
How do you usually handle a situation such as this?
What M-QB principle or thoughts could you apply to handle it better or differently?

Situation 2

One of the programs rules is that anyone late to meetings will have to run gassers before practice begins. One of your closest friends and teammates has been late a few times during the week, and you have noticed him quietly sneak into the film sessions through the back door without the coach noticing. In one of the meetings he sneaks into, the coach turns around and asks if he has been in the meeting the whole time. Your close friend and teammate lies and tells the coach that he has been in the film session the whole time. Nobody speaks up, too afraid to cause problems. He has gotten away with being late to meetings again, and this time also lied to the coach.

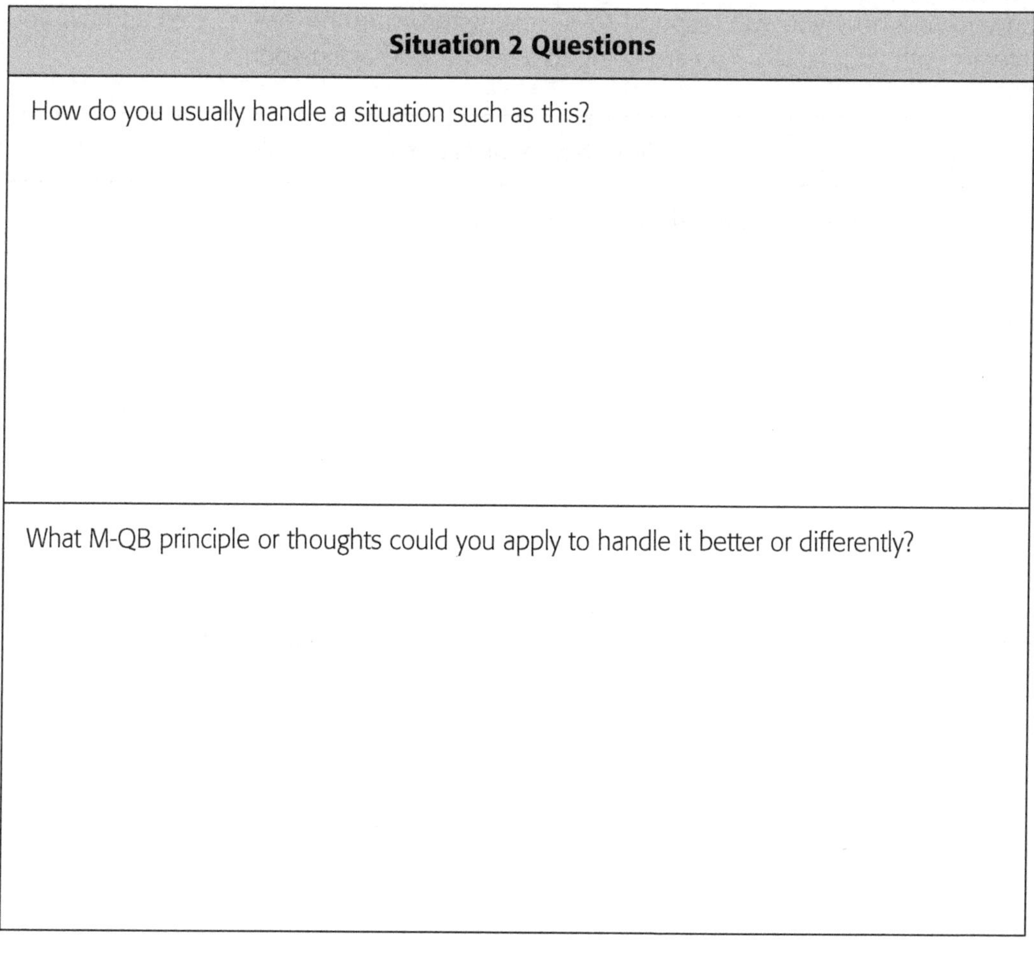

Situation 2 Questions
How do you usually handle a situation such as this?
What M-QB principle or thoughts could you apply to handle it better or differently?

Situation 3

You are not having a great night throwing the ball. You are missing easy throws, the velocity is lacking, and it is causing you to become frustrated with yourself and performance. You don't understand why things are not going well. You know how to throw the ball, you know the plays, and you keep messing up. Your coach tries to communicate with you on the sideline about what you need to do to better perform, and he is also irritated with the results. You feel he is coming down on you pretty hard, and you are beginning to allow what he is saying to frustrate you also. Your mind begins to think about your stats and college scouts watching the game. It is loud in the stands, you're in a competitive game still, and you know everyone has their eyes on you and how you will respond to adversity, throwing the ball as well as how you interact with your coach. You are going to take the field again soon.

Situation 3 Questions
How do you usually handle a situation such as this?
What M-QB principle or thoughts could you apply to handle it better or differently?

Situation 4

A young freshman or rookie is working extremely hard at practice. In your eyes, he has truly outworked all of the newcomers and even a handful of veterans all throughout camp. You can see he that he is working to be more than average and so that someone will notice him, but he remains quiet, focused, and does not want to ask for more reps or playing time because he does not want to look selfish. You truly believe his work is genuine and that he is being overlooked. Even the coaches might be overlooking this young player that could contribute to the team's success. You notice that he could compete with some of the starting players for their spot if given the chance, but no one notices him, and when he asks for help to improve, none of the older player will help him. You want him to be recognized, but you might also be worried about creating a controversy with the older players.

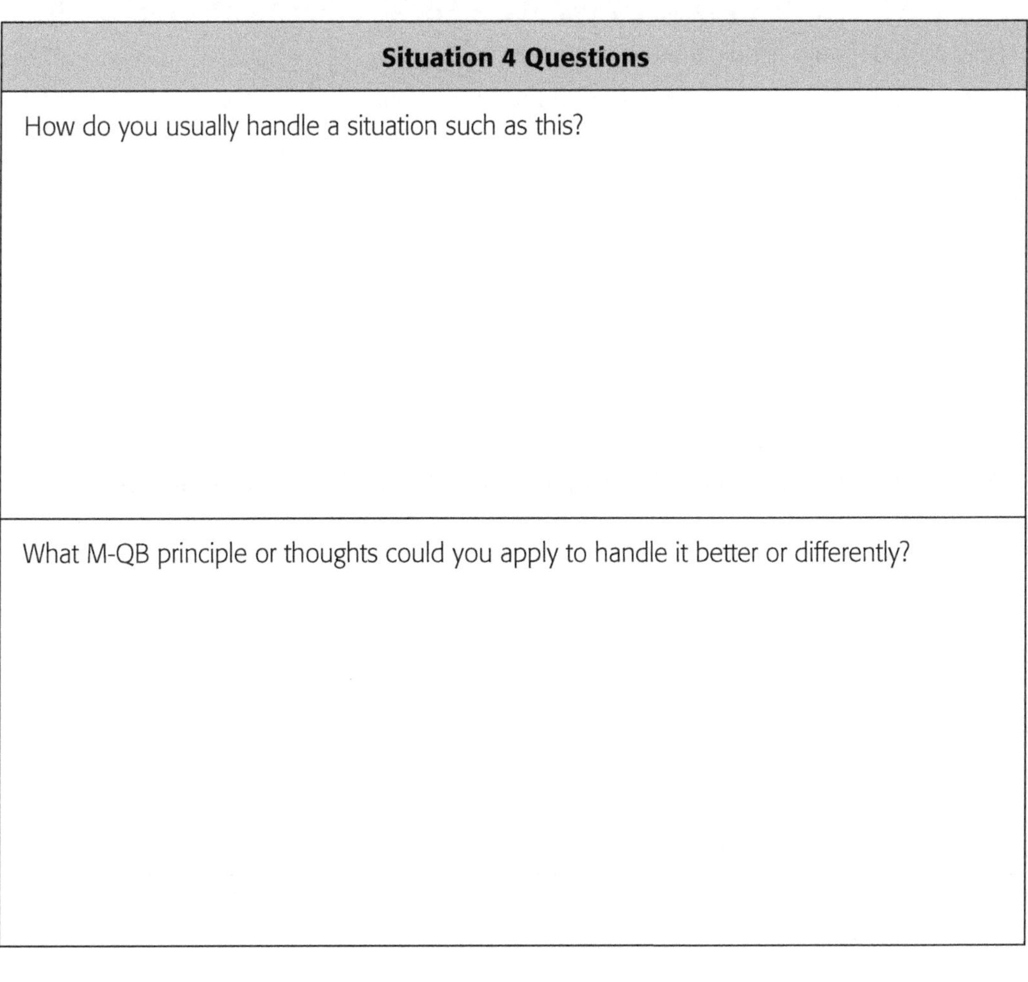

Situation 4 Questions
How do you usually handle a situation such as this?
What M-QB principle or thoughts could you apply to handle it better or differently?

Situation 5

You are heading out to practice and are finishing up your pre-practice mindful breathing exercises, and you notice that the tone of practice is dull. It is quiet, no one is talking, and everyone seems unmotivated to be at practice that day. Many of your teammates are heading out to practice complaining about another day of practice and how they cannot wait for it to be over. There is absolutely no energy or buzz in the air. This is football, a game, but it does not seem anyone is enjoying the process of preparing, and their body language and state of mind shows it. Everyone is just standing around and looking as if they are attending a funeral, and now you're about to go onto the practice field to join them.

Situation 5 Questions
How do you usually handle a situation such as this?
What M-QB principle or thoughts could you apply to handle it better or differently?

Situation 6

It's early in an important game, and already things are not going the team's way. To make it worse, you are getting hit every single time you drop back to throw a pass and barely have time to set your feet. You are the visiting team in a hostile environment, and the crowd cheers at every mishap you have as a Quarterback. It's not getting any easier as you begin to hear boos and disapproval from your own fans that made the trip over. You begin to lose your cool, anger is setting in, and everything about you begins to unravel. Your mind is racing about losing, your heart rate is increasing, and your breathing is rapid and heavy. You want so bad to get back onto the field so you can show everyone that you are not out of it yet, but you have to wait until you get the ball back on offense. You stand on the sideline waiting and watch as the opposing team marches into the end zone. You're about to take the field again.

Situation 6 Questions
How do you usually handle a situation such as this?
What M-QB principle or thoughts could you apply to handle it better or differently?

APPENDIX A
Extras

Appendix A-1: M-QB Guided Imagery

Note: This script can be read by the coach to the Quarterback, or the Quarterback can read it to himself. I encourage that coaches and Quarterbacks also create their own situations to envision success.

Setting

You're the home team on a beautiful, cool night. The stadium is packed. You're on the sideline late in the game, hoping to get the ball back one last time. The crowd is a bit restless, as they know the opposing offense is doing all they can to run out the clock. You are sitting on the bench relaxing, breathing, and hoping that the defense will make a stop and give you one more chance to win. You keep to yourself as third down approaches, still praying for a defensive stop. You can barely watch as you stay sitting, Breathing calmly, just looking at the ground. Seconds later, you hear your home crowd erupt with a loud cheer, and see your coach running over to the official calling for a timeout, which is your final one. You stand up, grab your helmet, and watch the opposing team punt the ball away. You put your helmet on, buckle your chinstrap, get the first play call from your coach, and jog out to the huddle. You look at every one of your teammates, and they are all business! No words need to be said; the mission is clear. You give them the play and break the huddle. It's go time!

Game Situation

- Score: Down 20-24
- Quarter: Fourth
- Time Left: 1:18
- Timeouts: 0
- Yards to Go: 70

The Drive

You line up in shotgun with a spread formation. You take a moment to see the field as the defense begins to get aligned. You receive the snap and drop back. Your offensive line provides great pass protection and a pocket for you to step up and throw downfield. As you scan the field, you see your slot receiver break past the linebackers on a skinny post and complete a strike to him just as he makes his break. You gain huge yardage and get just past midfield. You have no time-outs, you quickly look to the sideline as you are running to where the ball is spotted, and your coach signals the next play. You relay the play to everyone as quickly as possible as time has just ticked below one minute remaining. You quickly relax your mind and take the next snap. The offensive line is playing amazingly, you have all day to throw, and you trust the process, protection, and your progressions. Right as you complete you drop, you see the slot receiver from your left come open on a crossing route, and you throw him the ball to the perfect location where only he can grab it and keep running. He gains big yards and gets to around the 30-yard line. Time is still ticking as you gain another first down. You look to the sideline, and your coach is signaling for you to spike the ball to stop the clock. You begin yelling to your team to get set as time is running down. You get under center quickly, take the snap, and spike the ball to stop the clock. The clock has stopped, and the entire stadium is into the game and on the edge of their seat, but you don't notice any of those things. You are locked into the present, and you quickly observe your body and mind. You have a moment before the next play to calm your adrenaline and shift your mind to paying attention to the task at hand. Your teammates are breathing heavily, but still locked in. No one has the energy to talk; simple head nods to each other are enough to know that everyone is on the same page.

The ref signals to resume play; you have time to make sure everyone is properly aligned because the clock has stopped. It's now second down with just under 30 seconds remaining. You signal for the snap and quickly complete a short pass to your outside receiver. He tries to get out-of-bounds, but the defender takes him to the ground before he can get to the sideline. You know time is running out and without hesitation line everyone up to spike the ball, which you do quickly. It is now third down with 15 seconds remaining in the game. You quickly jog over to the sideline, and your coach reminds you that you cannot take sack and that the rest of the plays need to be passes to the end zone. He gives you the call; you jog back to the huddle and give the play call. You line up, take a deep breath, and signal for the snap. When you receive the snap, you are calm, cool, and collected as you have been the whole drive. The offensive line is protecting you to perfection. Your finish your drop, settle in to your body, and deliver a fade pass down the sideline and into the end zone. You watch the play develop slowly and with curiosity, wondering what's about to happen. The wide receiver jumps to go after the ball, which is thrown just over the defender's hand and bring it into his body for a touchdown! No flags on the field; it's a touchdown! You are instantly rushed by your offensive linemen, who could crush you with their enthusiasm. You embrace them, and you all run into the end zone to celebrate with your teammates who just made a beautiful catch. There are only six seconds remaining, and with the made extra point your team now leads 27-24. The fans in the stadium are losing their minds with excitement and cannot believe what they just witnessed. You remain focused as you watch the final kickoff happen and the opposing team is unable to answer. The game is over; your team wins. It was a courageous effort by all.

Appendix A-2: Seeing the Field

My hope is that this exercise will assist Quarterbacks in being fully present before they take each snap. Oftentimes, the poor decisions a Quarterback happen because he does not take his time to truly see the field before he signals for the snap. He might glance, look around for a little bit, and go through the checks of the defense, but he is not just doing so in robotic fashion. The mind should be clear before the Quarterback takes each snap. What Mindful Quarterbacking teaches is approaching the line of scrimmage (LOS) very similar to how a professional golfer approaches the tee before he pulls back and rips the ball down the fairway. The same patience, calmness, focus, and intentions that a professional golfer displays before his swing is the same focus a Quarterback should have and practice before taking a snap and executing the play. In golf, a quiet environment is encouraged at all times. In football, noise is encouraged at all times, but the Quarterback now has the tools to help ignore or fade out the noise, remain calm, and keep his focus so he will be able to approach the line of scrimmage similar to how a professional golfer approached the tee.

Quarterback Exercise

When you begin to approach the line of scrimmage, take whatever breath you have in you and use either the inbreath to absorb it into the body or the outbreath to completely release it (whatever feels right or comes natural) and begin with a new breath, slowly inviting the inbreath and patiently allowing the outbreath to makes its way. Take your eyes through your pre-snap progressions and see everything for what it truly is by allowing your eyes to perform the thinking process, giving your mind pure information rather than allowing your mind to be given information from your imagination.

Now begin to feel the focus coming into your eyes, mind, and body and settle into the moment. When you are settled, you should now be able to better execute the next snap because your eyes and mind are clear and your body relaxed. There is nothing interfering with what you know. You know the play, you know the defense, and you know your progressions and assignment. The noise is gone, the sidelines in your peripheral vision are gone, and the imagination from the mind is gone. The only thing your mind sees is what you are about to accomplish in this moment when the ball is snapped.

When you signal for the ball, the auto self will begin to do its job without interruption because the mind and body are in a pure state. As you go through your progression (assuming it's a pass), do so with soft, open eyes but with purpose. The football is gently nested in your grip and secure because you've already become familiar through object awareness; it's natural. Now that your his eyes have identified the situation, let the ball go to its destination, let it fly without worry or fear, and observe what happens. Repeat this process for each play.

This process is to help you maximize your abilities that you've already obtained through hard work and film study. You cannot simply do this without working hard. The more you study, the better this process will help you. If you are struggling, it will help you improve. If you are performing great, this can help you enhance and build on what you're already doing well. The game is moving faster around you than anyone else, and you need to respond quickly, but do so by allowing your eyes and the auto-self (not your imagination) to do its job. If you do that, you'll execute with the timing and precision you need, and the game around you will appear to slow down, allowing you to perform at a higher level.

Appendix A-3: Dealing With Pain

There are some situations where a Quarterback must play through the pain he's experiencing. Playing through pain is a choice, and it is one that should be made intelligently by finding out by a medical trainer or doctor if it's okay to continue playing. If so, and he chooses to play through the pain, the following tips/advice on how to do so utilizing mindfulness will be helpful.

Tips for Quarterbacks

- *Be kind to yourself and those helping you:* Far too often, people who are in pain allow the pain to impact every part of their life in that moment. Have compassion toward yourself, and show gratitude and kindness for those trying to assist you. Pain is temporary. You can handle it.
- *Take a minute to sit with the pain:* When you're in pain, the first trained response is to be upset with the fact that you were inflicted with pain in the first place. Depending on what happened, you might place all of your emotions into the pain you're experiencing because your imagination is causing your mind to think worst-case scenario. When you experience pain, try to sit with it after the initial shock and allow it to be what it is. The severity of the pain and pain thresholds vary, but try not let it become more than what is actually going on. There is nothing wrong with being in pain or responding to pain; just live with what is actually present not what you're thinking it to be.
- *Don't take pain personally:* Pain is a part of life; everyone goes through it in some capacity. Try not to associate pain with punishment. Even though you're the one in pain at that time, try to remember that people in this world are going through pain every second of the day and also possibly worse than what you're experiencing at that time. Try to shift your mind from "Why does this have to happen to me?" to "I am in pain, and this is not ideal. I wish I wasn't, but I can get through this; many people have." Use the pain you're experiencing as a challenge and one that you can overcome.

Appendix A-4: Unwelcoming Weather

I hear players every single year say; "Every kind of weather is football weather." I will say about 80 percent of those guys would prefer a nice, clear day and the perfect amount of sunshine every day of the week. Outside of college football or professional football, where weather can really come to your advantage because of teams traveling to unfamiliar conditions all over the country, most coaches prefer nice weather, too. Outside of those circumstances that give us an advantage to win, deep down we all wish it was beautiful and sunny every week, However, in a lot of places, that is not going to be the case, and there are a few things I believe players can do to still perform well in bad weather, and no position needs it more than the Quarterback because, again, the ball is always in his hands.

Tips for Quarterbacks

- *Acceptance:* It is what it is. You have no control over what the weather is going to be like, and the weather doesn't care about what you think. You cannot stop it, so you might as well welcome it with open arms and an open heart.
- *Enthusiasm:* Almost all of us, despite competitive advantages, want to play in nice weather, however what separates teams who perform well in bad conditions from teams who play poorly is the enthusiastic approach. Get pumped up about it! It's still football; you're not going out in that weather doing nothing! Every type of weather is football weather. Even as a coach, I pump myself up to go outside, it's fun!
- *Competitive:* Look at unwelcoming weather as a challenge rather than as a setback. When you walk outside and it's blazing hot or freezing cold, take it head on, and refuse to be denied. Along with accepting the conditions for what they are, remaining competitive and even displaying courage will help you deal with whatever the elements are. You just have to be properly prepared.
- *Preparation:* Being prepared for unwelcoming weather conditions is an absolute must. It might sound like basic information or common sense, but most problems that happen with performance in unwelcoming weather happens because of lack of preparation before and during competition.
  - ✓ *Wet Weather:* Use the common wet ball drill. Take a bucket of water, place the footballs in there and throw with them during practice. I advise that you don't try to overadjust throwing the football, keep it the same, and let your authentic throwing abilities takeover. You will naturally adjust without thinking about it. Just throw.
  - ✓ *Freezing/Snow:* Do the same thing as above except place the wet footballs in a freezer throughout the day. If needed, re-inflate them just before you use them because the air pressure will naturally drop. Use these types of footballs during any running period in practice. It will help you get familiar with gripping the cold and very slick surface. You can also incorporate object awareness with these types of footballs–something a few of my Quarterbacks have done and have had success with.

- ✓ *Extreme Heat:* Mindful breathing and hydration is best for when the heat really cranks up. When it's very hot, mindful breathing can help cool the body, regulate blood flow, and clear the mind. If you hydrate as you should, eat as you should, and apply mindful breathing, you will find you begin to deal with beating the heat as you do any other distraction.

With everything listed in this section, it's important that you always dress properly for the elements. Do not try to brave the cold and showoff how tough you are and do not underestimate the heat and overdress. It doesn't help. Lastly, expect the unexpected and always bring extra layers, lighter layers, gloves, cleats, socks, etc. You never know what the weather wants to challenge you with. Be prepared!

APPENDIX B
Quarterback Preparation Tools

Note: If he chooses, the Quarterback may take this playbook with him to practice and fill out his three element goals or to remind himself of what he chose before practice begins. He can also respond to how his pre-practice meditations went. He can respond to the daily reflection log and the reflection questions immediately after practice or later on that day if he chooses.

Approaching Practice

- B-1: Three Elements Pre-Practice Goal Sheet
- B-2: Pre-Practice Meditations
- B-3: Practice Reflection Sheet
- B-4: Practice Reflection Question Sheet

Approaching Game Time

- B-5: M-QB Pre-Game Routine
- B-6: Game-Time Self-Evaluation Sheet
- B-7: Game-Time Reflection Sheet

Appendix B-1: Three Elements Pre-Practice Goal Sheet

Three Elements Pre-Practice Goal Sheet		
Week ____	**Week ____**	**Week ____**
Monday	**Monday**	**Monday**
Intention	Intention	Intention
Attention	Attention	Attention
Attitude	Attitude	Attitude
Tuesday	**Tuesday**	**Tuesday**
Intention	Intention	Intention
Attention	Attention	Attention
Attitude	Attitude	Attitude
Wednesday	**Wednesday**	**Wednesday**
Intention	Intention	Intention
Attention	Attention	Attention
Attitude	Attitude	Attitude
Thursday	**Thursday**	**Thursday**
Intention	Intention	Intention
Attention	Attention	Attention
Attitude	Attitude	Attitude

Appendix B-2: Pre-Practice Meditations

Monday

Mindful Breathing

Just before practice is about to begin, find somewhere outside (preferably) to comfortably sit (or inside, if necessary). Make this location your home base for your pre-practice meditations. It is more than okay to switch up the location, but many prefer to have a spot of home for their meditation practice. Either decision is perfectly okay. You can choose to sit on the ground, on a cushion you bring, a bench, or anywhere you feel comfortable. As you sit down, you can sit with your legs crossed or by simply being comfortable the way you are. Sit upright, with a sense of relaxed authority, not too relaxed, but not too stiff either. Next, gently set your hands into your lap if your legs are crossed, or gently on your knees if you're sitting on a bench or chair, and let your hands and arms simply be relaxed. Take a moment to simply be where you are, and bring your mind to simply be as still as your body in this moment. When you feel you have reached a comfortable feeling of stillness, slowly close your eyes as gently as possible.

Slowly begin to breathe in and out for about five to six seconds at a time, through the nose and out the nose or mouth. Allow the inbreath (inhale) to happen naturally without force, and allow it to make its journey into your body and settle where it sees fit.

Next, when the inbreath has settled, slowly release the outbreath (exhale) through the nostrils or the mouth with gentleness and without force. When you begin to feel your chest relax, slowly come back to the inbreath and repeat the breathing cycle.

You may feel the urge after a few repetitions to take a deep breath, allowing the inbreath to make its way deep into the body. Take advantage of the deep inbreath, and when it settles deeply, hold briefly, and identify the feeling, comfort, and energy the deep inbreath provides, and allow the outbreath to make its way back out of the body. Do this starting for a couple of minutes and try to add a minute or two each week.

Monday Meditation Experience

Use this page to check the box the best describes the feeling you had after your Monday meditation. You will check the box once a week. After checking the box you choose, compare your daily reflection from practice that day. This is so you can track your progression and gain an understanding of your emotions each day of the week throughout the season and how you felt heading into practice and how it may or may not have impacted the intention, attention, and attitude you chose that day.

Feeling After Monday Meditation	*Great*	*Good*	*Alright*	*Nothing*
Week 1				
Week 2				
Week 3				
Week 4				
Week 5				
Week 6				
Week 7				
Week 8				
Week 9				
Week 10				
Week 11				
Week 12				
Week 13				
Week 14				
Week 15				
Week 16				
Week 17				
Week 18				

Tuesday

Mindful Awareness

This section is to assist you in enhancing your awareness of your surroundings and help you better experience the simple things you do every day before practice that get overlooked. You can perform this exercise while doing just about anything; you can sit or stand still, but it is not necessary.

When you're on your way into the locker room or practice field, shift your mindset to wanting to pay attention on purpose to the environment. You might want to pay attention to the sounds of the lockers opening and shutting, the sounds of the cleats on the concrete outside, the blended noise, laughter, and the smells.

Next, choose something within that environment to pay attention to on purpose with full awareness. Whatever you choose to be your intention, give the experience and object or events of focus your full attention.

While doing this, have an attitude of being non-judgmental and just allowing things to unfold naturally as they are without any interference, and allow the experience to unfold like watching a film. Perhaps you've chosen to pay attention to the laughter in the locker room and the smiles on faces, and you begin to gain a sense of gratitude and appreciation. If an experience such as this arises, just live in the experience and absorb the moment for what it truly is.

Hold the experience in with gentle eyes, and if and when you remember, you can slowly bring the inbreath and the outbreath to your experience—not changing anything, just allowing the breath to find it's rhythm with the experience.

Feel free to be creative when performing this meditation. Also feel free to stick with objects or events that work best for you, but creativity is encouraged. Always remember that you can apply these meditations anytime and anywhere in life.

Tuesday Meditation Experience

Use this page to check the box the best describes the feeling you had after your Tuesday meditation. You will check the box once a week. After checking the box you choose, compare your daily reflection from practice that day. This is so you can track your progression and gain an understanding of your emotions each day of the week throughout the season and how you felt heading into practice and how it may or may not have impacted the intention, attention, and attitude you chose that day.

Feeling After Tuesday Meditation	*Great*	*Good*	*Alright*	*Nothing*
Week 1				
Week 2				
Week 3				
Week 4				
Week 5				
Week 6				
Week 7				
Week 8				
Week 9				
Week 10				
Week 11				
Week 12				
Week 13				
Week 14				
Week 15				
Week 16				
Week 17				
Week 18				

Wednesday

Object Awareness

To assist with enhancing touch, feel, and familiarity with the football, you can practice with other objects away from the field, but coming into practice, utilize the football because you will be with a football at all times during the course of the season. Most Quarterbacks I've worked with find that this meditation helps bring them feeling closer to the game and take them into a "go time" mindset. This can be done while walking or sitting and can be worked on throughout practice as well. Quarterbacks I have worked with also feel that it enhances their awareness of ball security. Grab a football, and hold in your hands effortlessly. Whether you are walking or sitting, toss the ball lightly from one hand to the other, gently allowing the weight of the ball to come to rest in each hand. As you go back and forth, when you are ready, bring your attention to the way the grip or laces feel on your fingertips as you release and receive the ball in each hand. While you release the ball, also listen for any sounds that may come from the football leaving one hand and into the other.

Next, hold the football with both hands, and observe its texture, color, and shape. Look at any symbols, logos, or odd marks on the ball, and simply observe them with curiosity.

Last, gently close your eyes and begin rotating the ball in your hands, bringing your attention to the way the football feels. How does the grip pattern feel? Is it smooth, rough, or in between? Notice if you effortlessly begin to grip the football the way you normally do when you throw it. You can also slowly bring in the inbreath and the outbreath along with you while you do this.

Something you can add is to bring the football with you wherever you go on the field or off and see how often you bring your attention to the fact you're holding a football in your hands or arm and how often you go through the day carrying it without noticing.

Wednesday Meditation Experience

Use this page to check the box the best describes the feeling you had after your Wednesday meditation. You will check the box once a week. After checking the box you choose, compare your daily reflection from practice that day. This is so you can track your progression and gain an understanding of your emotions each day of the week throughout the season and how you felt heading into practice and how it may or may not have impacted the intention, attention, and attitude you chose that day.

Feeling After Wednesday Meditation	*Great*	*Good*	*Alright*	*Nothing*
Week 1				
Week 2				
Week 3				
Week 4				
Week 5				
Week 6				
Week 7				
Week 8				
Week 9				
Week 10				
Week 11				
Week 12				
Week 13				
Week 14				
Week 15				
Week 16				
Week 17				
Week 18				

Thursday

Noise (Stadium) Awareness

This is a simple drill I've used with my Quarterbacks. Almost everyone today has technology where they can listen to music whenever and wherever they want. What I have my Quarterbacks do is listen to loud stadium noise in their headphones the day before the game during pre-practice and at times during particular parts of practice. This exercise has been helpful and oftentimes give the Quarterback a boost, knowing that they've already worked with noise leading up to the game. A lot of programs have simulated stadium noise for their players for years; this is just another way of doing it.

Take your headphones with you out to the stadium, put them in, and turn up the volume of the crowd noise you selected. Begin walking from the locker room and onto the field.

Next, walk onto the field, and stop after 10 yards while listening to the sounds coming into your ears. Slowly look up into the empty stands, and imagine the scene of both the home and away fans and their faces, boos, cheers, taunts, and such. For a moment, observe the feelings in your body. Is your heart rate up? Is your breathing becoming heavier or quicker? Is the adrenaline rush from your mind really beginning to pick up?

Continue to advance upfield, and stop every 10 yards; this time, keep your eyes forward into the other end zone the rest of the way, and repeat the process of observing your body and emotions. Remember to use non-judging when it comes to the way you receive the noise and maybe have an attitude of acceptance because you cannot control the external environment around you. Identify how often you keep your mind on advancing 10 yards without your mind being distracted by thoughts of crowd noise.

Last, when you get to the other end zone, take a minute to remember your journey. Were you mostly in the experience or in the crowd? As you head back to the locker room, go the entire distance without stopping, keeping your eyes forward and without the noise this time.

Thursday Meditation Experience

Use this page to check the box that best describes the feeling you had after your Thursday meditation. You will check the box once a week. After checking the box you choose, compare your daily reflection from practice that day. This is so you can track your progression and gain an understanding of your emotions each day of the week throughout the season and how you felt heading into practice and how it may or may not have impacted the intention, attention, and attitude you chose that day.

Feeling After Thursday Meditation	*Great*	*Good*	*Alright*	*Nothing*
Week 1				
Week 2				
Week 3				
Week 4				
Week 5				
Week 6				
Week 7				
Week 8				
Week 9				
Week 10				
Week 11				
Week 12				
Week 13				
Week 14				
Week 15				
Week 16				
Week 17				
Week 18				

Appendix B-3: Practice Reflection Sheet

Week ____: Practice Reflection Sheet
Monday
Tuesday
Wednesday
Thursday

Appendix B-4: Practice Reflection Question Sheet

The Quarterback can write down his responses to the following questions on his own paper, or he can simply reflect on the questions and answer them to himself. Writing down responses in a notebook or on these sheets is recommended.

Practice Reflection Question Sheet
What principles did you apply today?
Why did you choose those principles?
Did any of the principles you chose come into use today? How?
What went well for you and/or the team today at practice?
Do you feel you were fully present during practice today?
What do you remember most from practice today?
What internal or external distractions came up during practice?
What did you do to handle any distractions or issues that arose?
Did you meet your intention(s) today?
Did you pay full attention to what you wanted?
Did you bring and maintain the attitude you wanted?
Did you give your absolute best efforts today?
What do you want to improve on?
What do you want to continue to do well?
(Final practice of the week question) Overall, do you feel you made improvements as a Quarterback this week? In what areas?

Appendix B-5: M-QB Pre-Game Routine

Following is a routine for quarterbacks to follow when preparing mentally the day of a game. There are many different ways to prepare; this is the approach I have had my Quarterbacks utilize and what has worked best in my experience. The very first thing for the quarterback to do is to try to encompass every pre-practice meditation that was used throughout the week/season.

Pre-Game Routine for Quarterbacks

You might want to begin coming into your pre-game routine by utilizing the mindful awareness that morning and bringing your full attention to the environment surrounding game time that morning and living in a sense of excitement and gratitude for the fact that you're getting ready to play the game you love today. You can use the mindful awareness on your way to school, the locker room, the stadium, and the bus if you have to hit the road. Utilizing mindful awareness will help you relax while remaining focused and keep your mind at ease by allowing the gratitude of your surroundings and the game to pass through you, rather than allowing your imagination to run wild and creating a false sense of reality and worry.

When it comes to mindful breathing, I tend to have my Quarterbacks begin getting into their routine about three or four hours before kickoff. The reason they begin so early is that you want to be fully in routine by the time you reach the stadium so that your mind and body is fully relaxed by the time you reach the stadium. You do not want to feel rushed in your breathing, so the sooner you begin, the better. I've had Quarterbacks start the night before the game and continue up to kickoff; it's a preference. So by this point you'll have a clear mind and gratitude with mindful awareness and a relaxed mind and body with mindful breathing. That's a good combination before arriving to the stadium.

When you get to the stadium and enter the locker room, keep everything you have going with your mindful awareness and mindful breathing routine; by this time, you might have entered a state of flow, and it's not even something you need to think about, it's just happening. Find a spot in the locker room where you can sit and relax, and bring in object awareness with a football. Doing so will very slowly bring your mind to the game. While maintaining your current state of being, simply bring your mind to the objective and allow your now-clear mind to envision success similar to the M-QB guided meditation. Allow your thoughts to pass through, not responding to them, and simply observing the emotions that come through you, while maintaining the natural flow of the inbreath and the outbreath. By this time, your mind is clear of any distractions, your breathing should be flowing, and your body relaxed and in command of itself as you head out onto the field.

When you get out onto the field, utilize noise awareness with the current game day environment. If you're able, you can go through the same routine you do weekly, or simply be in the present moment and observe the way your mind and body processes the environment. Your mind should be clear, your body relaxed with your mind on the objective. The noise is now just simply there with no impact whatsoever.

During team stretch or the walkthrough period, simply stretch and execute with the present moment awareness you have.

Your intention to be fully present is accomplished. Your attention is fully on the game, and your attitude can be whatever you want it to be at that time because you are in the now and ready for kickoff.

This routine, if utilized and practiced consistently, will no doubt help bring you into your zone and help you perform one snap at a time. There will be obstacles and distractions during games that will try to take you out of your zone, but you will have the tools to combat any distractions that come your way so you can focus, perform to the best of your abilities, and help give your team the greatest chance of being successful.

As a side note, I strongly advise utilizing these meditations on the sideline throughout the course of a game and just adapt based on the environment around you. I find my Quarterbacks have had the best results using mindful breathing when they need to regroup themselves. They utilize mindful awareness when anger or frustration sets in. They use object awareness to bring their mind back to the game and task at hand, and they use noise awareness when they become distracted. Being consistent in your routine will also help train the mind and body to more quickly identify exactly what you're trying to accomplish. Utilizing mindful breathing, mindful awareness, object awareness, and noise awareness meditations can be useful individually for multiple situations and can also be combined in various ways to help troubleshoot whatever challenges arise. Many Quarterbacks end up making these meditations their own, and that is a great thing! "It's all about the now."

Appendix B-6: Game Time Self-Evaluation Sheet

Game ______: M-QB Game Time Self-Evaluation Sheet				
M-QB Principle	The Whole Time	Most of the Time	Some of the Time	Not at All
Coachable				
Communication				
Confidence				
Calmness				
Consistency				
Control				
Competitive				
Courage				
Compassion				

Appendix B-7: Game Time Reflection Sheet

The Quarterback can write down his responses on his own paper, or he may simply reflect on the questions and answer them to himself. Writing down responses in a notebook or on these sheets is recommended.

Game ______: M-QB Game Time Reflection Questions
Did you meet your goals?
Did any of the Cs of Competition come into use today? How?
What M-QB or custom principles did you apply?
Why did you choose those principles?
What during the game went well for you and/or the team?
Do you feel you were fully present during the game?
What do you remember most from the game today?
What internal or external distractions came up during the game?
What did you do to handle any distractions or issues that arose?
Did you pay full attention to what you wanted?
Did you bring and maintain the attitude you wanted?
Did you give your absolute best efforts?
What principles do you want to apply next time?
What can you do to build on or improve your performance?
Overall thoughts and reflection from the game?

ABOUT THE AUTHOR

Marcus Mayo has been coaching football for more than 10 years at multiple levels. His first coaching experience was spending a season working with youth players in his home city, Virginia Beach, Virginia. Marcus played Quarterback in high school and was at the junior college level (Rock Valley College) for a brief period before ultimately deciding to turn his attention to coaching full-time.

Since then, Marcus has made a career out of coaching, working his way into high school and the college ranks, coaching multiple positions on both sides of the ball. Marcus has coached high school football in Rockford, Illinois and Missoula, Montana. He started his college career as a student assistant coach and video coordinator at NAIA Rocky Mountain College (MT) and since then has coached at NCAA Division II South Dakota School of Mines and his most recent stop, NAIA Carroll College (MT).

Marcus has brought the mindful coaching approach with him throughout his career, applying it to multiple positions. Marcus is the founder of Mindful Quarterbacking where he trains Quarterbacks and merges the practice and concepts of mindfulness with the art of Quarterbacking to help players maximize their potential on and off the field. Marcus applies his mindfulness studies and practice to everyday life and his coaching career, along with teaching mindfulness to others. Marcus most recently expanded his mindfulness teaching techniques and approach by completing the Mindful Educator Essentials program with Mindful Schools. He is looking forward to applying the mindful coaching approach throughout the rest of his coaching career and hopes that other coaches and educators will adopt mindfulness principles into their coaching to help athletes at all levels reach their fullest potential on and off the field.

Marcus is proud to have been raised in a United States Navy family and considers Virginia and Maryland his home. He considers Missoula, Montana, his second home. Marcus graduated from the University of Montana with a degree in liberal/religious studies. A large amount of his work was focused on South and Southeast Asian studies and the study of mindfulness and the benefits of applying mindfulness qualities to any part of life, including athletic performance. He is a member of the American Football Coaches Association.